FIVE
LESSONS

FIVE
LESSONS

A MASTER CLASS
BY NEVILLE

Includes Bonus
Questions & Answers

NEVILLE GODDARD

Published 2020 by Gildan Media LLC
aka G&D Media
www.GandDmedia.com

Front cover design by David Rheinhardt of Pyrographx

Interior design by Meghan Day Healey of Story Horse, LLC

Library of Congress Cataloging-in-Publication Data is available upon request

ISBN: 978-1-7225-0356-7

10   9   8   7   6   5   4   3   2   1

PUBLISHER'S NOTE

Neville Goddard (1905–1972) delivered a series of five lessons in Los Angeles in 1948. This copy reproduces Neville's complete presentations, together with the question and answer session.

CONTENTS

Lesson 1

CONSCIOUSNESS IS THE ONLY REALITY

This is going to be a very practical course. Therefore, I hope that everyone in this class has a very clear picture of what he desires, for I am convinced that you can realize your desires by the technique you will receive here this week in these five lessons.

That you may receive the full benefit of these instructions, let me state now that the Bible has no reference at all to any persons who ever existed, or to any event that ever occurred upon earth.

The ancient storytellers were not writing history but an allegorical picture lesson of certain basic principles, which they clothed in the garb of history, and they adapted these stories to the limited capacity of a most uncritical and credulous people.

Throughout the centuries we have mistakenly taken personifications for persons, allegory for history, the vehicle that conveyed the instruction for the instruction, and the gross first sense for the ultimate sense intended.

The difference between the form of the Bible and its substance is as great as the difference between a grain of corn and the life-germ within that grain. As our assimilative organs discriminate between food that can be built into our system and food that must be discarded, so do our awakened intuitive faculties discover beneath allegory and parable, the psychological life-germ of the Bible; and, feeding on this, we, too, cast off the form which conveyed the message.

The argument against the historicity of the Bible is too lengthy; consequently, it is not suitable for inclusion in this practical psychological interpretation of its stories. Therefore, I will waste no time in trying to convince you that the Bible is not an historical fact.

Tonight I will take four stories and show you what the ancient storytellers intended that you and I should see in these stories. The ancient teachers attached psychological truths to phallic and solar allegories. They did not know as much of the physical structure of man as do modern scientists, neither did they know as much about the heavens as do our modern astronomers. But the little they did know they used wisely and they built phallic and solar frames to which they tied the great psychological truths that they had discovered.

In the Old Testament you will find much of the phallic worship. Because it is not helpful, I am not going to emphasize it. I shall only show you how to interpret it.

Before we come to the first of the psychological dramas that you and I may use in a practical sense, let me state the two outstanding names of the Bible: the one you and I translate as GOD or JEHOVAH, and the one we call his son, which we have as JESUS.

The ancients spelled these names by using little symbols. The ancient tongue, called the Hebraic language, was not a tongue that you exploded with the breath. It was a mystical language never uttered by man. Those who understood it, understood it as mathematicians understand symbols of higher mathematics. It is not something people used to convey thought as I now use the English language.

They said that God's name was spelled, YOD HEY VAV HEY. I shall take these symbols and in our normal, down-to-earth language, explain them in this manner.

The first letter, YUD in the name GOD is a hand or a seed, not just a hand, but the hand of the director. If there is one organ of man that discriminates and sets him apart from the entire world of creation it is his hand. What we call a hand in the anthropoid ape is not a hand. It is used only for the purpose of conveying food to the mouth, or to swing from branch to branch. Man's hand fashions, it molds. You cannot really express yourself without the hand. This is the builder's hand, the hand of the director; it directs and molds and builds within your world.

The ancient storytellers called the first letter YUD, the hand, or the absolute seed out of which the whole of creation will come.

To the second letter, HEY, they gave the symbol of a window. A window is an eye—the window is to the house what the eye is to the body.

The third letter, VAV, they called a nail. A nail is used for the purpose of binding things together. The conjunction "and" in the Hebraic tongue is simply the third letter, or VAV. If I want to say "man and woman", I put the VAV in the middle, it binds them together.

The fourth and last letter, HEY, is another window or eye.

In this modern, down-to-earth language of ours, you can forget eyes and windows and hands and look at it in this manner. You are seated here now. This first letter, YUD, is your I AMness, your awareness. You are aware of being aware—that is the first letter. Out of this awareness all states of awareness come.

The second letter, HEY, called an eye, is your imagination, your ability to perceive. You imagine or perceive something which seems to be other than Self. As though you were lost in reverie and contemplated mental states in a detached manner, making the thinker and his thoughts separate entities.

The third letter, VAV, is your ability to feel you are that which you desire to be. As you feel you are it, you become aware of being it. To walk as though you were what you want to be is to take your desire out of the imaginary world and put the VAV upon it. You have completed the drama of creation. I am aware of something. Then I become aware of actually being that of which I was aware.

The fourth and last letter in the name of God is another HEY, another eye, meaning the visible objective world which constantly bears witness of that which I am conscious of being. You do nothing about the objective world; it always molds itself in harmony with that which you are conscious of being

You are told this is the name by which all things are made, and without it there is nothing made that is made. The name is simply what you have now as you are seated here. You are conscious of being, aren't you? Certainly you are. You are also conscious of something that is other than yourself: the room, the furniture, the people.

You may become selective now. Maybe you do not want to be other than what you are, or to own what you see. But you have the capacity to feel what it would be like were you now other than what you are. As you assume that you are that which you want to be, you have completed the name of God or the YUD HEY VAV HEY. The final result, the objectification of your assumption, is not your concern. It will come into view automatically as you assume the consciousness of being it.

Now let us turn to the Son's name, for he gives the Son dominion over the world. You are that Son, you are the great Joshua, or Jesus, of the Bible. You know the name Joshua or Jehoshua we have Anglicized as Jesus.

The Son's name is almost like the Father's name. The first three letters of the Father's name are the first three letters of the Son's name, YUD HEY VAV, then you add a SHIN and an AYIN, making the Son's name read, YUD HEY VAV SHIN AYIN'.

You have heard what the first three are: YUD HEY VAV. YUD means that you are aware; HEY means that you are aware of something; and VAV means that you became aware of being that of which you were aware. You have dominion because you have the ability to conceive and to become that which you conceive. That is the power of creation.

But why is a SHIN put in the name of the Son? Because of the infinite mercy of our Father. Mind you, the Father and the Son are one. But when the Father becomes conscious of being man he puts within the condition called man that which he did not give unto himself. He puts a SHIN for this purpose: a SHIN is symbolized as a tooth.

A tooth is that which consumes, that which devours. I must have within me the power to consume that which I now dislike.

I, in my ignorance, brought to birth certain things I now dislike and would like to leave behind me. Were there not within me the flames that would consume it, I would be condemned forever to live in a world of all my mistakes. But there is a SHIN, or flame, within the name of the Son, which allows that Son to become detached from states He formerly expressed within the world. Man is incapable of seeing other than the contents of his own consciousness.

If I now become detached in consciousness from this room by turning my attention away from it, then, I am no longer conscious of it. There is something in me that devours it within me. It can only live within my objective world if I keep it alive within my consciousness.

It is the SHIN, or a tooth, in the Son's name that gives him absolute dominion. Why could it not have been in the Father's name? For this simple reason: Nothing can cease to be in the Father. Even the unlovely things cannot cease to be. If I once give it expression, forever and ever it remains locked within the dimensionally greater Self which is the Father. But I would not like to keep alive within my world all of my mistakes. So I, in my infinite mercy gave to myself, when I became man, the power to become detached from these things that I, in my ignorance, brought to birth in my world..

These are the two names which give you dominion. You have dominion if, as you walk the earth, you know that your consciousness is God, the one and only reality. You become aware of something you would like to express or possess. You have the ability to feel that you are and possess that which but a moment before was imaginary. The final result, the embodying of your assumption, is completely outside of the offices of a three-dimensional mind. It comes to birth in a way that no man knows.

If these two names are clear in your mind's eye, you will see that they are your eternal names. As you sit here, you are this YUD HEY VAV HEY; you are the YUD HEY VAV SHIN AYIN.

The stories of the Bible concern themselves exclusively with the power of imagination. They are really dramatizations of the technique of prayer, for prayer is the secret of changing the future. The Bible reveals the key by which man enters a dimensionally larger world for the purpose of changing the conditions of the lesser world in which he lives.

A prayer granted implies that something is done in consequence of the prayer, which otherwise would not have been done. Therefore, man is the spring of action, the directing mind, and the one who grants the prayer.

The stories of the Bible contain a powerful challenge to the thinking capacity of man. The underlying truth—that they are psychological dramas and not historical facts—demands reiteration, inasmuch as it is the only justification for the stories. With a little imagination we may easily trace the psychological sense in all the stories of the Bible.

"And God said, Let us make man in our image, and after our likeness: and let them have dominion over the fish of the sea, and over the fowl of the air, and over the cattle, and over all the earth, and over every creeping thing that creepeth upon the earth. So God created man in his own image, in the image of God created he him" Gen. 1:26, 27.

Here in the first chapter of the Bible the ancient teachers laid the foundation that God and man are one, and that man has dominion over all the earth. If God and man are one, then God can never be so far off as even to be near, for nearness implies separation.

The question arises: What is God? God is man's consciousness, his awareness, his I AMness. The drama of life is a psychological one in which we bring circumstances to pass by our attitudes rather than by our acts. The cornerstone on which all things are based is man's concept of himself. He acts as he does, and has the experiences that he does, because his concept of himself is what it is, and for no other reason. Had he a different concept of himself, he would act differently and have different experiences.

Man, by assuming the feeling of his wish fulfilled, alters his future in harmony with his assumption, for, assumptions though false, if sustained, will harden into fact.

The undisciplined mind finds it difficult to assume a state which is denied by the senses. But the ancient teachers discovered that sleep, or a state akin to sleep, aided man in making his assumption. Therefore, they dramatized the first creative act of man as one in which man was in a profound sleep. This not only sets the pattern for all future creative acts, but shows us that man has but one substance that is truly his to use in creating his world and that is himself.

"And the Lord God (man) caused a deep sleep to fall upon Adam and he slept: and he took one of his ribs, and closed up the flesh instead thereof; and the rib, which the Lord God had taken from man, made he a woman." Gen. 2: 21, 22.

Before God fashions this woman for man he brings unto Adam the beasts of the field, and the fowls of the air and has Adam name them. "Whatsoever Adam called every living creature, that was the name thereof."

If you will take a concordance or a Bible dictionary and look up the word thigh as used in this story you will see that it has nothing to do with the thigh. It is defined as the soft parts that are creative in a man, that hang upon the thigh of a man.

The ancient storytellers used this phallic frame to reveal a great psychological truth. An angel is a messenger of God. You are God, as you have just discovered for your consciousness is God, and you have an idea, a message. You are wrestling with an idea, for you do not know that you are already that which you contemplate, neither do you believe you could become it. You would like to, but you do not believe you could.

Who wrestles with the angel? Jacob. And the word Jacob, by definition, means the supplanter.

You would like to transform yourself and become that which reason and your senses deny. As you wrestle with your ideal, trying to feel that you are it, this is what happens. When you actually feel that you are it, something goes out of you. You may use the words, "Who has touched me, for I perceive virtue has gone out of me?"

You become for a moment, after a successful meditation, incapable of continuing in the act, as though it were a physical creative act. You are just as impotent after you have prayed successfully as you are after the physical creative act. When satisfaction is yours, you no longer hunger for it. If the hunger persists you did not explode the idea within you, you did not actually succeed in becoming conscious of being that which you wanted to be. There was still that thirst when you came out of the deep.

If I can feel that I am that which but a few seconds ago I knew I was not, but desired to be, then I am no longer hungry to be it. I am no longer thirsty because I feel satisfied in that state. Then something shrinks within me, not physically but in my feeling, in my consciousness, for that is the creativeness of man. He so shrinks in desire, he loses the desire to continue in this meditation. He does not halt physically, he simply has no desire to continue the meditative act.

"When you pray believe that you have received, and you shall receive." When the physical creative act is completed, the sinew which is upon the hollow of man's thigh shrinks, and man finds himself impotent or is halted. In like manner when a man prays successfully he believes that he is already that which he desired to be, therefore he cannot continue desiring to be that which he is already conscious of being. At the moment of satisfaction, physical and psychological, something goes out which in time bears witness to man's creative power.

Our next story is in the 38th chapter of the book of Genesis. Here is a king whose name is Judah, the first three letters of whose name also begins YUD HEY VAV. Tamar is his daughter-in-law.

The word Tarmar means a palm tree or the most beautiful, the most comely. She is gracious and beautiful to look on and is called a palm tree. A tall, stately palm tree blossoms even in the desert—wherever it is there is an oasis. When you see the palm tree in the desert, there will be found what you seek most in that parched land. There is nothing more desirable to a man moving across a desert than the sight of a palm tree.

In our case, to be practical, our objective is the palm tree. That is the stately, beautiful one that we seek.

Whatever it is that you and I want, what we truly desire, is personified in the story as Tamar the beautiful.

We are told she dresses herself in the veils of a harlot and sits in the public place. Her father-in-law, King Judah, comes by; and he is so in love with this one who is veiled that he offers her a kid to be intimate with her.

She said, "What will you give me as a pledge that you will give me a kid?"

Looking around he said, "What do you want me to give as a pledge?"

She answered, "Give me your ring, give me your bracelets, and give me your staff."

Whereupon, he took from his hand the ring, and the bracelet, and gave them to her along with his sceptre. And he went in unto her and knew her, and she bore him a son.

That is the story; now for the interpretation. Man has one gift that is truly his to give, and that is himself. He has no other gift, as told you in the very first creative act of Adam be getting the woman out of himself. There was no other substance in the world but himself with which he could fashion the object of his desire. In like manner Judah had but one gift that was truly his to give—himself, as the ring, the bracelets, and the staff symbolized, for these were the symbols of his kingship.

Man offers that which is not himself, but life demands that he give the one thing that symbolizes himself. "Give me your ring, give me your bracelet, give me your sceptre." These make the king. When he gives them he gives of himself.

You are the great King Judah. Before you can know your Tamar and make her bear your likeness in the world, you must go in unto her and give of self. Suppose I want security. I cannot get it by knowing people who have it. I cannot get it by pulling strings. I must become conscious of being secure.

Let us say I want to be healthy. Pills will not do it. Diet or climate will not do it. I must become conscious of being healthy by assuming the feeling of being healthy.

Perhaps I want to be lifted up in this world. Merely looking at kings and presidents and noble people and living in their reflection will not make me dignified. I must become conscious of being noble and dignified and walk as though I were that which I now want to be.

When I walk in that light I give of myself to the image that haunted my mind, and in time she bears me a child; which means I objectify a world in harmony with that which I am conscious of being.

You are King Judah and you are also Tamar. When you become conscious of being that which you want to be you are Tamar. Then you crystallize your desire within the world round about you.

No matter what stories you read in the Bible, no matter how many characters these ancient storytellers introduced into the drama, there is one thing you and I must always bear in mind—they all take place within the min of the individual man. All the characters live in the mind of the individual man.

As you read the story, make it fit the pattern of self. Know that your consciousness is the only reality. Then know what you want to be. Then assume the feeling of being that which you want to be, and remain faithful to your assumption, living and acting on your conviction. Always make it fit that pattern.

Our third interpretation is the story of Isaac and his two sons: Esau and Jacob. The picture is drawn of a blind man being deceived by his second son into giving him the blessing which belonged to his first son. The story stresses the point that the deception was accomplished through the sense of touch.

"And Isaac said unto Jacob, Come near, I pray thee that I may feel thee, my son, whether thou be my very son Esau or not. And Jacob went near unto Isaac his father; and he felt him. . . . And it came to pass, as soon as Isaac had made an end of blessing Jacob, and Jacob was yet scarce gone out from the presence of Isaac his father, that Esau his brother came in from his hunting." Gen. 27:21, 30.

This story can be very helpful if you will reenact it now. Again bear in mind that all the characters of the Bible are personifications of abstract ideas and must be fulfilled in the individual man. You are the blind father and both sons.

Isaac is old and blind, and sensing the approach of death, calls his first son Esau a rough hairy boy, and sends him into the woods that he may bring in some venison.

The second son, Jacob, a smooth skin boy, overheard the request of his father. Desiring the birthright of his brother, Jacob, the smooth skinned son, slaughtered one of his father's flock and skinned it. Then, dressed in the hairy skins of the kid he had slaughtered, he came through subtlety and betrayed his father into believing that he was Esau.

The father said, "Come close my son that I may feel you. I cannot see, but come that I may feel." Note the stress that is placed upon feeling in this story.

He came close and the father said to him, "The voice is Jacob's voice, but the hands are the hands of Esau." And feeling this roughness, the reality of the son Esau, he pronounced the blessing and gave it to Jacob.

You are told in the story that as Isaac pronounced the blessing and Jacob had scarcely gone out from his presence, that his brother Esau came in from his hunting.

This is an important verse. Do not become distressed in our practical approach to it, for as you sit here you, too, are Isaac. This room in which you are seated is your present Esau. This is the rough or sensibly known world, known by reason of your bodily organs. All of your senses bear witness to the fact that you are here in this room. Everything tells you that you are here, but perhaps you do not want to be here.

You can apply this toward any objective. The room in which you are seated at any time—the environment in which you are placed, this is your rough or sensibly known world or son which is personified in the story as Esau. What you would like in place of what you have or are is your smooth skinned state or Jacob, the supplanter.

You do not send your visible world hunting, as so many people do, by denial. By saying it does not exist you make it all the more real. Instead, you simply remove your attention from the region of sensation which at this moment is the room round about you, and you concentrate your attention on that which you want to put in its place, that which you want to make real.

In concentrating on your objective, the secret is to bring it here. You must make elsewhere here and then now imagine that your objective is so close that you can feel it.

Suppose at this very moment I want a piano here in this room. To see a piano in my mind's eye existing elsewhere does not do it. But to visualize it in this room as though it were here and to put my mental hand upon the piano and to feel it solidly real, is to take that subjective state personified as my second son Jacob and bring it so close that I can feel it.

Isaac is called a blind man. You are blind because you do not see your objective with your bodily organs, you cannot see it with your objective senses. You only perceive it with your mind, but you bring it so close that you can feel it as though it were solidly real now. When this is done and you lose yourself in its reality and feel it to be real, open your eyes.

When you open your eyes what happens? The room that you had shut out but a moment ago returns from the hunt. You no sooner gave the blessing—felt the imaginary state to be real—than the objective world, which seemingly was unreal, returns. It does not speak to you with words as recorded of Esau, but the very room round about you tells you by its presence that you have been self-deceived.

It tells you that when you lost yourself in contemplation, feeling that you were now what you wanted to be, feeling that you now possess what you desire to possess, that you were simply deceiving self. Look at this room. It denies that you are elsewhere.

If you know the law, you now say: "Even though your brother came through subtlety and betrayed me and took your birthright, I gave him your blessing and I cannot retract."

In other words, you remain faithful to this subjective reality and you do not take back from it the power of birth. You gave it the right of birth and it is going to become objective within this world of yours. There is no room in this limited space of yours for two things to occupy the same space at the same time. By making the subjective real it resurrects itself within your world.

Take the idea that you want to embody, and assume that you are already it. Lose yourself in feeling this assumption is solidly real. As you give it this sense of reality, you have given it the blessing which belongs to the objective world, and you do not have to aid its birth any more than you have to aid the birth of a child or a seed you plant in the ground. The seed you plant grows unaided by a man, for it contains within itself all the power and all the plans necessary for self-expression.

You can this night re-enact the drama of Isaac blessing his second son and see what happens in the immediate future in your world. Your present environment vanishes, all the circumstances of life change and make way for the coming of that to which you have given your life. As you walk, knowing that you are what you wanted to be, you objectify it without the assistance of another.

The fourth story for tonight is taken from the last of the books attributed to Moses. If you need proof that Moses did not write it, read the story carefully. It is found in the 34th chapter of the book of Deuteronomy. Ask any priest or rabbi, "who is the author of this book?", and they will tell you that Moses wrote it.

In the 34th chapter of Deuteronomy you will read of a man writing his own obituary, that is, Moses wrote this chapter. A man may sit down and write what he would like to have placed upon his tombstone, but here is a man who writes his own obituary. And then he dies and so completely rubs himself out that he defies posterity to find where he has buried himself.

"So Moses the servant of the Lord died there in the land of Moab, according to the word of the Lord. And he buried him in a valley in the land of Moab, over against Beth-Peor: but no man knoweth of his sepulchre unto this day. And Moses was an hundred and twenty years old when he died: his eye was not dim, nor his natural force abated." Deut. 34:5, 6,7.

You must this night—not tomorrow—learn the technique of writing your own obituary and so completely die to what you are that no man in this world can tell you where you buried the old man. If you are now ill and you become well, and I know you by reason of the fact that you are ill, where can you point and tell me you buried the sick one?

If you are impoverished and borrow from every friend you have, and then suddenly you roll in wealth, where did you bury the poor man? You so completely rub out poverty in your mind's eye that there is nothing in this world you can point to and claim, "that is where I left it". A complete transformation of consciousness rubs out all evidence that anything other than this ever existed in the world.

The most beautiful technique for the realizing of man's objective is given in the first verse of the 34th chapter of Deuteronomy: "And Moses went up from the Plains of Moab unto the mountain of Nebo, to the top of Pisgah, that is over against Jericho. And the Lord shewed him all the land of Gilead, unto Dan."

You read that verse and say, "So what?" But take a concordance and look up the words. The first word, Moses, means to draw out, to rescue, to lift out, to fetch. In other words, Moses is the personification of the power in man that can draw out of man that which he seeks, for everything comes from within, not from without. You draw from within yourself that which you now want to express as something objective to yourself.

You are Moses coming out of the plains of Moab. The word Moab is a contraction of two Hebraic words, Mem and Ab, meaning mother-father. Your consciousness is the mother-father there is no other cause in the world. Your I AMness, your awareness, is this Moab or mother-father. You are always drawing something out of it.

The next word is Nebo. In your concordance Nebo is defined as a prophecy. A prophecy is something subjective. If I say, "So-and-so will be," it is an image in the mind; it is not yet a fact. We must wait and either prove or disprove this prophecy.

In our language Nebo is your wish, your desire. It is called a mountain because it is something that appears difficult to ascend and is therefore seemingly impossible of realization. A mountain is something bigger than you are, it towers over you. Nebo personifies that which you want to be in contrast to that which you are.

The word Pisgah, by definition, is to contemplate. Jericho is a fragrant odor. And Gilead means the hills of witnesses. The last word is Dan the Prophet.

Now put them all together in a practical sense and see what the ancients tried to tell us. As I stand here, having discovered that my consciousness is God, and that I can by simply feeling that I am what I want to be transform myself into the likeness of that which I am assuming I am; I know now that I am all that it takes to scale this mountain.

I define my objective. I do not call it Nebo, I call it my desire. Whatever I want, that is my Nebo, that is my great mountain that I am going to scale. I now begin to contemplate it, for I shall climb to the peak of Pisgah.

I must contemplate my objective in such a manner that I get the reaction that satisfies. If I do not get the reaction that pleases then Jericho is not seen, for Jericho is a fragrant odor. When I feel that I am what I want to be I cannot suppress the joy that comes with that feeling.

I must always contemplate my objective until I get the feeling of satisfaction personified as Jericho. Then I do nothing to make it visible in my world; for the hills of Gilead, meaning men, women, children, the whole vast world round about me, come bearing witness. They come to testify that I am what I have assumed myself to be, and am sustaining within myself. When my world conforms to my assumption the prophecy is fulfilled.

If I now know what I want to be, and assume that I am it, and walk as though I were, I become it and becoming it I so completely die to my former concept of self that I cannot point to any place in this world and say: that is where my former self is buried. I so completely died that I defy posterity to ever find where I buried my old self.

There must be someone in this room who will so completely transform himself in this world that his close immediate circle of friends will not recognize him.

For ten years I was a dancer, dancing in Broadway shows, in vaudeville, night clubs, and in Europe. There was a time in my life when I thought I could not live without certain friends in my world. I would spread a table every night after the theater and we would all dine well. I thought I could never live without them. Now I confess I could not live with them. We have nothing in common today. When we meet we do not purposely walk on the opposite side of the street, but it is almost a cold meeting because we have nothing to discuss. I so died to that life that as I meet these people they cannot even talk of the old times.

But there are people living today who are still living in that state, getting poorer and poorer. They always like to talk about the old times. They never buried that man at all, he is very much alive within their world.

Moses was 120 years, a full, wonderful age as 120 indicates. One plus two plus zero equals three, the numerical symbol of expression. I am fully conscious of my expression. My eyes are undimmed and the natural functions of my body are not abated. I am fully conscious of being what I do not want to be.

But knowing this law by which a man transforms himself, I assume that I am what I want to be and walk in the assumption that it is done. In becoming it, the old man dies and all that was related to that former concept of self dies with it. You cannot take any part of the old man into the new man. You cannot put new wine in old bottles or new patches on old garments. You must be a new being completely.

As you assume that you are what you want to be, you do not need the assistance of another to make it so. Neither do you need the assistance of anyone to bury the old man for you. Let the dead bury the dead. Do not even look back, for no man having put his hand to the plow and then looking back is fit for the kingdom of heaven.

Do not ask yourself how this thing is going to be. It does not matter if your reason denies it. It does not matter if all the world round about you denies it. You do not have to bury the old. "Let the dead bury the dead." You will so bury the past by remaining faithful to your new concept of Self that you will defy the whole vast future to find where you buried it. To this day no man in all of Israel has discovered the sepulchre of Moses.

These are the four stories I promised you tonight. You must apply them every day of your life. Even though the chair on which you are now seated seems hard and does not lend itself to meditation you can, by imagination, make it the most comfortable chair in the world.

Let me now define the technique as I want you to employ it. I trust each one of you came here tonight with a clear picture of your desire. Do not say it is impossible. Do you want it? You do not have to use your moral code to realize it. It is altogether outside the reach of your code.

Consciousness is the one and only reality. Therefore, we must form the object of our desire out of our own consciousness.

People have a habit of slighting the importance of simple things, and the suggestion to create a state akin to sleep in order to aid you in assuming that which reason and your senses deny, is one of the simple things you might slight.

However, this simple formula for changing the future, which was discovered by the ancient teachers and given to us in the Bible, can be proved by all.

The first step in changing the future is Desire, that is, define your objective—know definitely what you want.

Second: construct an event which you believe you would encounter FOLLOWING the fulfillment of your desire—an event which implies fulfillment of your desire—something which will have the action of Self predominant.

The third step is to immobilize the physical body and induce a state akin to sleep. Then mentally feel yourself right into the proposed action, imagine all the while that you are actually performing the action HERE AND NOW. You must participate in the imaginary action, not merely stand back and look on, but FEEL that you are actually performing the action, so that the imaginary sensation is real to you.

It is important always to remember that the proposed action must be one which FOLLOWS the fulfillment of your desire, one which implies fulfillment. For example, suppose you desired promotion in office. Then being congratulated would be an event you would encounter following the fulfillment of your desire.

Having selected this action as the one you will experience in imagination to imply promotion in office, immobilize your physical body and induce a state bordering on sleep, a drowsy state, but one in which you are still able to control the direction of your thoughts, a state in which you are attentive without effort. Then visualize a friend standing before you. Put your imaginary hand into his. Feel it to be solid and real, and carry on an imaginary conversation with him in harmony with the FEELING OF HAVING BEEN PROMOTED.

You do not visualize yourself at a distance in point of space and at a distance in point of time being congratulated on your good fortune. Instead, you MAKE elsewhere HERE and the future NOW. The difference between FEELING yourself in action, here and now, and visualizing yourself in action, as though you were on a motion-picture screen, is the difference between success and failure.

The difference will be appreciated if you will now visualize yourself climbing a ladder. Then, with eyelids closed imagine that a ladder is right in front of you and FEEL YOURSELF ACTUALLY CLIMBING IT.

Experience has taught me to restrict the imaginary action which implies fulfillment of the desire, to condense the idea into a single act, and to re-enact it over and over again until it has the feeling of reality. Otherwise, your attention will wander off along an associational track, and hosts of associated images will be presented to your attention, and in a few seconds they will lead you hundreds of miles away from your objective in point of space and years away in point of time.

If you decide to climb a particular flight of stairs, because that is the likely event to follow the fulfillment of your desire, then you must restrict the action to climbing that particular flight of stairs. Should your attention wander off, bring it back to its task of climbing that flight of stairs, and keep on doing so until the imaginary action has all the solidity and distinctness of reality.

The idea must be maintained in the mind without any sensible effort on your part. You must, with the minimum of effort permeate the mind with the feeling of the wish fulfilled.

Drowsiness facilitates change because it favors attention without effort, but it must not be pushed to the state of sleep in which you no longer are able to control the movements of your attention. But a moderate degree of drowsiness in which you are still able to direct your thoughts.

A most effective way to embody a desire is to assume the feeling of the wish fulfilled and then, in a relaxed and drowsy state, repeat over and over again like a lullaby, any short phrase which implies fulfillment of your desire, such as, "Thank you, thank you, thank you" as though you addressed a higher power for having given you that which you desired.

I know that when this course comes to an end on Friday many of you here will be able to tell me you have realized your objectives. Two weeks ago I left the platform and went to the door to shake hands with the audience. I am safe in saying that at least 35 out of a class of 135 told me that which they desired when they joined this class they had already realized. This happened only two weeks ago. I did nothing to bring it to pass save to give them this technique of prayer. You need do nothing to bring it to pass—save apply this technique of prayer.

With your eyes closed and your physical body immobilized induce a state akin to sleep and enter into the action as though you were an actor playing the part. Experience in imagination what you would experience in the flesh were you now in possession of your objective. Make elsewhere HERE and then NOW. And the greater you, using a larger focus will use all means, and call them good, which tend toward the production of that which you have assumed.

You are relieved of all responsibility to make it so, because as you imagine and feel that it is so your dimensionally larger self determines the means. Do not think for one moment that some one is going to be injured in order to make it so, or that some one is going to be disappointed. It is still not your concern. I must drive this home. Too many of us, schooled in different walks of life, are so concerned about the other.

You ask, "If I get what I want will it not imply injury to another?" There are ways you know not of, so do not be concerned.

Close your eyes now because we are going to be in a long silence. Soon you will become so lost in contemplation, feeling that you are what you want to be, that you will be totally unconscious of the fact that you are in this room with others.

You will receive a shock when you open your eyes and discover we are here. It should be a shock when you open your eyes and discover that you are not actually that which, a moment before, you felt you were, or felt you possessed. Now we will go into the deep.

SILENCE PERIOD.

I need not remind you that you are now that which you have assumed that you are. Do not discuss it with anyone, not even self. You cannot take thought as to the HOW, when you know that you ARE already.

Your three-dimensional reasoning, which is a very limited reasoning indeed should not be brought into this drama. It does not know. What you have just felt to be true is true.

Let no man tell you that you should not have it. What you feel that you have, you will have. And I promise you this much, after you have realized your objective, on reflection you will have to admit that this conscious reasoning mind of yours could never have devised the way.

You are that and have that which this very moment you appropriated. Do not discuss it. Do not look to someone for encouragement because the thing might not come. It has come. Go about your Father's business doing everything normally and let these things happen in your world.

ASSUMPTIONS HARDEN INTO FACT

This Bible of ours has nothing to do with history. Some of you may yet be inclined tonight to believe that, although we can give it a psychological interpretation, it still could be left in its present form and be interpreted literally. You cannot do it. The Bible has no reference at all to people or to events as you have been taught to believe. The sooner you begin to rub out that picture the better.

We are going to take a few stories tonight, and again I am going to remind you that you must re-enact all of these stories within your own mind.

Bear in mind that although they seem to be stories of people fully awake, the drama is really between you, the sleeping one, the deeper you, and the conscious waking you. They are personified as people, but when you come to the point of application you must remember the importance of the drowsy state.

All creation, as we told you last night, takes place in the state of sleep, or that state which is akin to sleep—the, sleepy drowsy state.

We told you last night the first man is not yet awakened. You are Adam, the first man, still in the profound sleep. The creative you is the fourth-dimensional you whose home is simply the state you enter when men call you asleep.

Our first story for tonight is found in the Gospel of John. As you hear it unfold before you, I want you to compare it in your mind's eye to the story you heard last night from the book of Genesis. The first book of the Bible, the book of Genesis, historians claim is the record of events which occurred on earth some 3,000 years before the events recorded in the book of John. I ask you to be rational about it and see if you do not think the same writer could have written both stories. You be the judge as to whether the same inspired man could not have told the same story and told it differently.

This is a very familiar story, the story of the trial of Jesus. In this Gospel of John it is recorded that Jesus was brought before Pontius Pilate, and the crowd clamored for his life, they wanted Jesus. Pilate turned to them and said: "But ye have a custom, that I should release unto you one at the Passover; will ye therefore that I release unto you the King of the Jews? Then cried they all again, saying, Not this man, but Barabbas. Now Barabbas was a robber." John 18:39, 40.

You are told that Pilate had no choice in the matter, he was only a judge interpreting law, and this was the law. The people had to be given that which they requested. Pilate could not release Jesus against the wishes of the crowd, and so he released Barabbas and gave unto them Jesus to be crucified.

Now bear in mind that your consciousness is God. There is no other God. And you are told that God has a son whose name is Jesus. If you will take the trouble to look up the word Barabbas in your concordance, you will see that it is a contraction of two Hebraic words: BAR, which means a daughter or son, or child, and ABBA, which means father. Barabbas is the son of the great father. And Jesus in the story is called the Saviour, the Son of the Father.

We have two sons in this story. And we have two sons in the story of Esau and Jacob. Bear in mind that Isaac was blind, and justice to be true must be blindfolded. Although in this case Pilate is not physically blind, the part given to Pilate implies that he is blind because he is a judge. On all the great law buildings of the world we see the lady or the man who represents justice as being blindfolded.

"Judge not according to the appearance, but judge righteous judgment." John 7:24.

Here we find Pilate is playing the same part as Isaac. There are two sons. All the characters as they appear in this story can apply to your own life. You have a son that is robbing you this very moment of that which you could be.

If you came to this meeting tonight conscious of wanting something, desiring something, you walked in the company of Barabbas.

For to desire is to confess that you do not now possess what you desire, and because all things are yours, you rob yourself by living in the state of desire. My saviour is my desire. As I want something I am looking into the eyes of my saviour. But if I continue wanting it, I deny my Jesus, my saviour, for as I want I confess I am not and "except ye believe that I AM He ye die in your sins." I cannot have and still continue to desire what I have. I may enjoy it, but I cannot continue wanting it.

Here is the story. This is the feast of the Passover. Something is going to change right now, something is going to passover. Man is incapable of passing over from one state of consciousness into another unless he releases from consciousness that which he now entertains, for it anchors him where he is.

You and I may go to physical feasts year after year as the sun enters the great sign of Aries, but it means nothing to the true mystical Passover. To keep the feast of the Passover, the psychological feast, I pass from one state of consciousness into another. I do it by releasing Barabbas, the thief and robber that robs me of that state which I could embody within my world.

The state I seek to embody is personified in the story as Jesus the Saviour. If I become what I want to be then I am saved from what I was. If I do not become it, I continue to keep locked within me a thief who robs me of being that which I could be.

These stories have no reference to any persons who lived nor to any event that ever occurred upon earth. These characters are everlasting characters in the mind of every man in the world. You and I perpetually keep alive either Barabbas or Jesus. You know at every moment of time who you are entertaining.

Do not condemn a crowd for clamoring that they should release Barabbas and crucify Jesus. It is not a crowd of people called Jews. They had nothing to do with it.

If we are wise, we too should clamor for the release of that state of mind that limits us from being what we want to be, that restricts us, that does not permit us to become the ideal that we seek and strive to attain in this world.

I am not saying that you are not tonight embodying Jesus. I only remind you, that if at this very moment you have an unfulfilled ambition, then you are entertaining that which denies the fulfillment of the ambition, and that which denies it is Barabbas.

To explain the mystical, psychological transformation known as the Passover, or the crossing over, you must now become identified with the ideal that you would serve, and you must remain faithful to the ideal. If you remain faithful to it, you not only crucify it by your faithfulness, but you resurrect it unaided by a man.

As the story goes, no man could rise early enough to roll away the stone. Unaided by a man the stone was removed, and what seemingly was dead and buried was resurrected unassisted by a man.

You walk in the consciousness of being that which you want to be, no one sees it as yet, but you do not need a man to roll away the problems and the obstacles of life in order to express that which you are conscious of being. That state has its own unique way of becoming embodied in this world, of becoming flesh that the whole world may touch it.

Now you can see the relationship between the story of Jesus and the story of Isaac and his two sons, where one transplanted the other, where one was called the Supplanter of the other. Why do you think those who compiled the sixty odd books of our Bible made Jacob the forefather of Jesus?

They took Jacob, who was called the Supplanter, and made him father of twelve, then they took Judah or praise, the fifth son and made him the forefather of Joseph, who is supposed to have fathered in some strange way this one called Jesus. Jesus must supplant Barabbas as Jacob must supplant and take the place of Esau.

Tonight you can sit right here and conduct the trial of your two sons, one of whom you want released. You can become the crowd who clamors for the release of the thief, and the judge who willingly releases Barabbas, and sentences Jesus to fill his place. He was crucified on Golgotha, the place of the skull, the seat of the imagination.

To experience the Passover or passage from the old to the new concept of self, you must release Barabbas, your present concept of self, which robs you of being that which you could be, and you must assume the new concept which you desire to express.

The best way to do this is to concentrate your attention upon the idea of identifying yourself with your ideal. Assume you are already that which you seek and your assumption, though false, if sustained, will harden into fact.

You will know when you have succeeded in releasing Barabbas, your old concept of self, and when you have successfully crucified Jesus, or fixed the new concept of self, by simply looking MENTALLY at the people you know. If you see them as you formerly saw them, you have not changed your concept of self, for all changes of concepts of self result in a changed relationship to your world.

We always seem to others an embodiment of the ideal we inspire. Therefore, in meditation, we must imagine that others see us as they would see us were we what we desire to be.

You can release Barabbas and crucify and resurrect Jesus if you will first define your ideal. Then relax in a comfortable arm chair, induce a state of consciousness akin to sleep and experience in imagination what you would experience in reality were you already that which you desire to be.

By this simple method of experiencing in imagination what you would experience in the flesh were you the embodiment of the ideal you serve, you release Barabbas who robbed you of your greatness, and you crucify and resurrect your saviour, or the ideal you desired to express.

Now let us turn to the story of Jesus in the garden of Gethsemane. Bear in mind that a garden is a properly prepared plot of ground, it is not a wasteland. You are preparing this ground called Gethsemane by coming here and studying and doing something about your mind. Spend some time daily in preparing your mind by reading good literature, listening to good music, and entering into conversations that ennoble.

We are told in the Epistles, "Whatsoever things are true, whatsoever things are honest, whatsoever things are just, whatsoever things are pure, whatsoever things are lovely, whatsoever things are of good report; if there be any virtue, and if there be any praise, think on these things." Phil. 4:8.

Continuing with our story, as told in the 18th chapter of John, Jesus is in the garden and suddenly a crowd begins to seek him. He is standing there in the dark and he says, "Whom seek ye?"

The spokesman called Judas answers and says, "We seek Jesus of Nazareth."

A voice answers, "I am He."

At this instant they all fall to the ground, thousands of them tumbled. That in itself should stop you right there and let you know it could not be a physical drama, because no one could be so bold in his claim that he is the one sought, that he could cause thousands who seek him to fall to the ground.

But the story tells us they all fell to the ground. Then when they regained their composure they asked the same question.

"Jesus answered, I have told you that I am He: if therefore ye seek me, let these go their way." John 18:8.

"Then said Jesus unto him, That thou doest, do quickly." John 13:27.

Judas, who has to do it quickly, goes out and commits suicide.

Now to the drama. You are in your garden of Gethsemane or prepared mind if you can, while you are in a state akin to sleep, control your attention and not let it wander away from its purpose. If you can do that you are definitely in the garden.

Very few people can sit quietly and not enter a reverie or a state of uncontrolled thinking. When you can restrict the mental action and remain faithful to your watch, not permitting your attention to wander all over the place, but hold it without effort within a limited field of presentation to the state you are contemplating, then you are definitely this disciplined presence in the garden of Gethsemane.

The suicide of Judas is nothing more than changing your concept of yourself. When you know what you want to be you have found your Jesus or saviour. When you assume that you are what you want to be you have died to your former concept of self (Judas committed suicide) and are now living as Jesus. You can become at will detached from the world round about you, and attached to that which you want to embody within your world.

Now that you have found me, now that you have found that which would save you from what you are, let go of that which you are and all that it represents in the world. Become completely detached from it. In other words, go out and commit suicide.

You completely die to what you formerly expressed in this world, and you now completely live to that which no one saw as true of you before. You are as though you had died by your own hand, as though you had committed suicide. You took your own life by becoming detached in consciousness from what you formerly kept alive, and you begin to live to that which you have discovered in your garden. You have found your saviour.

It is not men falling, not a man betraying another, but you detaching your attention, and refocusing your attention in an entirely new direction. From this moment on you walk as though you were that which you formerly wanted to be. Remaining faithful to your new concept of yourself you die or commit suicide. No one took your life, you laid it down yourself.

You must be able to see the relation of this to the death of Moses, where he so completely died that no one could find where he was buried. You must see the relationship of the death of Judas. He is not a man who betrayed a man called Jesus.

The word Judas is praise; it is Judah, to praise, to give thanks, to explode with joy. You do not explode with joy unless you are identified with the ideal you seek and want to embody in this world. When you become identified with the state you contemplate you cannot suppress your joy. It rises like the fragrant odor described as Jericho in the Old Testament.

I am trying to show you that the ancients told the same story in all the stories of the Bible. All that they are trying to tell us is how to become that which we want to be. And they imply in every story that we do not need the assistance of another. You do not need another to become now what you really want to be.

Now we turn to a strange story in the Old Testament; one that very few priests and rabbis will be bold enough to mention from their pulpits. Here is one who is going to receive the promise as you now receive it. His name is Jesus, only the ancients called him Joshua, Jehoshua Ben Nun, or saviour, son of the fish, the Saviour of the great deep. Nun means fish, and fish is the element of the deep, the profound ocean. Jehoshua means Jehovah saves, and Ben means the offspring or son of. So he was called the one who brought the fish age.

This story is in the 6th book of the Bible, the book of Joshua. A promise is made to Joshua as it is made to Jesus in the Anglicized form in the gospels of Matthew, Mark, Luke and John.

In the gospel of John, Jesus says, "All things whatsoever thou hast given me are of thee." John 17:7. "And all mine are thine, and thine are mine." John 17:10.

In the Old Testament in the book of Joshua it is said in these words: "Every place that the sole of your foot shall tread upon, that have I given unto you." Joshua 1:3.

It does not matter where it is; analyze the promise and see if you can accept it literally. It is not physically true but it is psychologically true. Wherever you can stand in this world mentally that you can realize.

Joshua is haunted by this promise that wherever he can place his foot (the foot is understanding), wherever the sole of his foot shall tread, that will be given unto him. He wants the most desirable state in the world, the fragrant city, the delightful state called Jericho.

He finds himself barred by the impassable walls of Jericho. He is on the outside, as you are now on the outside. You are functioning three-dimensionally and you cannot seem to reach the fourth-dimensional world where your present desire is already a concrete objective reality. You cannot seem to reach it because your senses bar you from it. Reason tells you it is impossible, all things round about you tell you it is not true.

Now you employ the services of a harlot and a spy, and her name is Rahab. The word Rahab simply means the spirit of the father. RACE means the breath or spirit, and AB the father. Hence we find that this harlot is the spirit of the father and the father is man's awareness of being aware, man's I AMness, man's consciousness.

Your capacity to feel is the great spirit of the father, and that capacity is Rahab in this story. She has two professions that of a spy and that of a harlot.

The profession of a spy is this: to travel secretly, to travel so quietly that you may not be detected. There is not a single physical spy in this world who can travel so quietly that he will be altogether unseen by others. He may be very wise in concealing his ways, and he may never be truly apprehended, but at every moment of time he runs the risk of being detected.

When you are sitting quietly with your thoughts, there is no man in the world so wise that he can look at you and tell you where you are mentally dwelling.

I can stand here and place myself in London. Knowing London quite well, I can close my eyes and assume that I am actually standing in London. If I remain within this state long enough, I will be able to surround myself with the environment of London as though it were a solid concrete objective fact.

Physically I am still here, but mentally I am thousands of miles away and I have made elsewhere here. I do not go there as a spy, I mentally make elsewhere here, and then now. You cannot see me dwelling there, so you think I have just gone to sleep and that I an still here in this world, this three-dimensional world that is now San Francisco. As far as I am physically concerned, I am here but no one can tell me where I am when I enter the moment of meditation.

Rahab's next profession was that of a harlot, which is to grant unto men what they ask of her without asking man's right to ask. If she be an absolute harlot, as her name implies, then she possesses all and can grant all that man asks of her. She is there to serve, and not to question man's right to seek what he seeks of her.

You have within you the capacity to appropriate a state without knowing the means that will be employed to realize that end and you assume the feeling of the wish fulfilled without having any of the talents that men claim you must possess in order to do so. When you appropriate it in consciousness you have employed the spy, and because you can embody that state within yourself by actually giving it to yourself, you are the harlot, for the harlot satisfies the man who seeks her.

You can satisfy self by appropriating the feeling that you are what you want to be. And this assumption though false, that is, although reason and the senses deny it, if persisted in will harden into fact. By actually embodying that which you have assumed you are, you have the capacity to become completely satisfied. Unless it becomes a tangible, concrete reality you will not be satisfied; you will be frustrated.

You are told in this story that when Rahab went into the city to conquer it, the command given to her was to enter the heart of the city, the heart of the matter, the very center of it, and there remain until I come. Do not go from house to house, do not leave the upper room of the house into which you enter. If you leave the house and there be blood upon your head, it is upon your head. But if you do not leave the house and there be blood, it shall be upon my head.

Rahab goes into the house, rises to the upper floor, and there she remains while the walls crumble. That is, we must keep a high mood if we would walk with the highest. In a very veiled manner, the story tells you that when the walls crumbled and Joshua entered, the only one who was saved in the city was the spy and the harlot whose name was Rahab.

This story tells what you can do in this world. You will never lose the capacity to place yourself elsewhere and make it here. You will never lose the ability to give unto yourself what you are bold enough to appropriate as true of self. It has nothing to do with the woman who played that part.

The explanation of the crumbling of the walls is simple. You are told that he blew upon the trumpet seven times and at the seventh blast the walls crumbled and he entered victoriously into the state that he sought.

Seven is a stillness, a rest, the Sabbath. It is the state when man is completely unmoved in his conviction that the thing is. When I can assume the feeling of my wish fulfilled and go to sleep, unconcerned, undisturbed, I am at rest mentally, and am keeping the Sabbath or am blowing the trumpet seven times. And when I reach that point the walls crumble. Circumstances alter then remold themselves in harmony with my assumption. As they crumble I resurrect that which I have appropriated within. The walls, the obstacles, the problems, crumble of their own weight if I can reach the point of stillness within me.

The man who can fix within his own mind's eye an idea, even though the world would deny it, if he remains faithful to that idea he will see it manifested. There is all the difference in the world between holding the idea, and being held by the idea. Become so dominated by an idea that it haunts the mind as though you were it. Then, regardless of what others may say, you are walking in the direction of your fixed attitude of mind. You are walking in the direction of the idea that dominates the mind.

As we told you last night, you have but one gift that is truly yours to give, and that is yourself. There is no other gift; you must press it out of yourself by an appropriation. It is there within you now for creation is finished. There is nothing to be that is not now. There is nothing to be created for all things are already yours, they are all finished.

Although man may not be able to stand physically upon a state, he can always stand mentally upon any desired state. By standing mentally I mean that you can now, this very moment, close your eyes and visualize a place other than your present one, and assume that you are actually there. You can FEEL this to be so real that upon opening your eyes you are amazed to find that you are not physically there.

This mental journey into the desired state, with its subsequent feeling of reality, is all that is necessary to bring about its fulfillment. Your dimensionally greater Self has ways that the lesser, or three-dimensional you, know not of. Furthermore, to the greater you, all means are good which promote the fulfillment of your assumption.

Remain in the mental state defined as your objective until it has the feeling of reality, and all the forces of heaven and earth will rush to aid its embodiment. Your greater Self will influence the actions and words of all who can be used to aid the production of your fixed mental attitude.

Now we turn to the book of Numbers and here we find a strange story. I trust that some of you have had this experience as described in the book of Numbers. They speak of the building of a tabernacle at the command of God; that God commanded Israel to build him a place of worship.

He gave them all the specifications of the tabernacle. It had to be an elongated, movable place of worship,
and it had to be covered with skin. Need you be told
anything more? Isn't that man?

"Know ye not that ye are the temple of God, and that
the Spirit of God dwelleth in you?" 1 Cor. 3:16.

There is no other temple. Not a temple made with
hands, but a temple eternal in the heavens. This temple
is elongated, and it is covered with skin, and it moves
across the desert.

"And on the day that the tabernacle was reared up
the cloud covered the tabernacle, namely, the tent of the
testimony: and at even there was upon the tabernacle as
it were the appearance of fire, until the morning. So it
was always: the cloud covered it by day, and the appearance of fire by night." Num.9:15,16.

The command given to Israel was to tarry until the
cloud ascended by day and the fire by night. "Whether it
were two days, or a month, or a year, that the cloud tar-
ried upon the tabernacle, remaining thereon, the children of Israel abode in their tents, and journeyed not:
but when it was taken up, they journeyed." Num. 9:22.

You know that you are the tabernacle, but you may
wonder, what is the cloud. In meditation many of you
must have seen it. In meditation, this cloud, like the sub-
soil waters of an artesian well, springs spontaneously to

your head and forms itself into pulsating, golden rings. Then, like a gentle river they flow from your head in a stream of living rings of gold.

In a meditative mood bordering on sleep the cloud ascends. It is in this drowsy state that you should assume that you are that which you desire to be, and that you have that which you seek, for the cloud will assume the form of your assumption and fashion a world in harmony with itself. The cloud is simply the garment of your consciousness, and where your consciousness is placed, there you will be in the flesh also.

This golden cloud comes in meditation. There is a certain point when you are approaching sleep that it is very, very thick, very liquid, and very much alive and pulsing. It begins to ascend as you reach the drowsy, meditative state, bordering on sleep. You do not strike the tabernacle; neither do you move it until the cloud begins to ascend.

The cloud always ascends when man approaches the drowsiness of sleep. For when a man goes to sleep, whether he knows it or not, he slips from a three-dimensional world into a fourth-dimensional world and that which is ascending is the consciousness of that man in a greater focus; it is a fourth-dimensional focus.

What you now see ascending is your greater self. When that begins to ascend you enter into the actual state of feeling you are what you want to be. That is the time you lull yourself into the mood of being what you want to be, by either experiencing in imagination what you would experience in reality were you already that which you want to be, or by repeating over and over again the phrase that implies you have already done what you want to do. A phrase such as, "Isn't it wonderful, isn't it wonderful," as though some wonderful thing had happened to you.

"In a dream, in a vision of the night, when deep sleep falleth upon men, in slumberings upon the bed. Then he openeth the ears of men, and sealeth their instruction." Job 33:15, 16.

Use wisely the interval preceding sleep. Assume the feeling of the wish fulfilled and go to sleep in this mood. At night, in a dimensionally larger world, when deep sleep falleth upon men, they see and play the parts that they will later on play on earth. And the drama is always in harmony with that which their dimensionally greater selves read and play through them. Our illusion of free will is but ignorance of the causes which make us act.

The sensation which dominates the mind of man as he falls asleep, though false, will harden into fact. Assuming the feeling of the wish fulfilled as we fall asleep, is the command to this embodying process saying to our mood, "Be thou actual." In this way we become through a natural process what we desire to be.

I can tell you dozens of personal experiences where it seemed impossible to go elsewhere, but by placing myself elsewhere mentally as I was about to go to sleep, circumstances changed quickly which compelled me to make the journey. I have done it across water by placing myself at night on my bed as though I slept where I wanted to be. As the days unfolded things began to mold themselves in harmony with that assumption and all things that must happen to compel my journey did happen. And I, in spite of myself, must make ready to go toward that place which I assumed I was in when I approached the deep of sleep.

As my cloud ascends I assume that I am now the man I want to be, or that I am already in the place where I want to visit. I sleep in that place now. Then life strikes the tabernacle, strikes my environment and reassembles my environment across seas or over land and reassembles it in the likeness of my assumption. It has nothing to do with men walking across a physical desert. The whole vast world round about you is a desert.

From the cradle to the grave you and I walk as though we walk the desert. But we have a living tabernacle wherein God dwells, and it is covered with a cloud which can and does ascend when we go to sleep or are in a state akin to sleep. Not necessarily in two days, it can ascend in two minutes. Why did they give you two days? If I now become the man I want to be, I may become dissatisfied tomorrow. I should at least give it a day before I decide to move on.

The Bible says in two days, a month, or a year: whenever you decide to move on with this tabernacle let the cloud ascend. As it ascends you start moving where the cloud is. The cloud is simply the garment of your consciousness, your assumption. Where the consciousness is placed you do not have to take the physical body; it gravitates there in spite of you. Things happen to compel you to move in the direction where you are consciously dwelling.

"In my Father's house are many mansions: if it were not so, I would have told you. I go to prepare a place for you. And if I go and prepare a place for you, I will come again, and receive you unto myself; that where I am, there ye may be also." John 14:2, 3.

The many mansions are the unnumbered states within your mind, for you are the house of God. In my Father's house are unnumbered concepts of self. You could not in eternity exhaust what you are capable of being.

If I sit quietly here and assume that I am elsewhere, I have gone and prepared a place. But if I open my eyes, the bilocation which I created vanishes and I am back here in the physical form that I left behind me as I went to prepare a place. But I prepared the place nevertheless and will in time dwell there physically.

You do not have to concern yourself with the ways and the means that will be employed to move you across space into that place where you have gone and mentally prepared it. Simply sit quietly, no matter where you are, and mentally actualize it.

But I give you warning, do not treat it lightly, for I am conscious of what it will do to people who treat it lightly. I treated it lightly once because I just wanted to get away, based only upon the temperature of the day. It was in the deep of winter in New York, and I so desired to be in the warm climate of the Indies, that I slept that night as though I slept under palm trees. Next morning when I awoke it was still very much winter.

I had no intentions of going to the Indies that year, but distressing news came which compelled me to make the journey. It was in the midst of war when ships were being sunk right and left, but I sailed out of New York on a ship 48 hours after I received this news. It was the only way I could get to Barbados, and I arrived just in time to see my mother and say a three-dimensional "good-bye" to her.

In spite of the fact that I had no intentions of going, the deeper Self watched where the great cloud descended.

I placed it in Barbados and this tabernacle (my body) had to go and make the journey to fulfill the command, "Wherever the sole of your foot shall tread that have I given unto you." Wherever the cloud descends in the desert, there you reassemble that tabernacle.

I sailed from New York at midnight on a ship without taking thought of submarines or anything else. I had to go. Things happened in a way that I could not have devised.

I warn you, do not treat it lightly. Do not say, "I will experiment and put myself in Labrador, just to see if it will work." You will go to your Labrador and then you will wonder why you ever came to this class. It will work if you dare assume the feeling of your wish fulfilled as you go to sleep.

Control your moods as you go to sleep. I cannot find any better way to describe this technique than to call it a "controlled waking dream." In a dream you lose control, but try preceding your sleep with a complete controlled waking dream, entering into it as you do in dream, for in a dream you are always very dominant, you always play the part. You are always an actor in a dream, and never the audience. When you have a controlled waking dream you are an actor and you enter into the act of the controlled dream. But do not do it lightly, for you must then reenact it physically in a three-dimensional world.

Now before we go into our moment of silence there is something I must make very clear, and that is this effort we discussed last night. If there is one reason in this whole vast world why people fail it is because they are unaware of a law known to psychologists today as the law of reverse effort.

When you assume the feeling of your wish fulfilled it is with a minimum of effort. You must control the direction of the movements of your attention. But you must do it with the least effort. If there is effort in the control, and you are compelling it in a certain way you are not going to get the results. You will get the opposite results, what ever they might be.

That is why we insist on establishing the basis of the Bible as Adam slept. That is the first creative act, and there is no record where he was ever awakened from this profound sleep. While he sleeps creation stops.

You change your future best when you are in control of your thoughts while in a state akin to sleep, for then effort is reduced to its minimum. Your attention seems to completely relax, and then you must practice holding your attention within that feeling, without using force, and without using effort.

Do not think for a moment that it is will power that does it. When you release Barabbas and become identified with Jesus, you do not will yourself to be it, you imagine that you are it. That is all you do.

Now as we come to the vital part of the evening, the interval devoted to prayer, let me again clarify the technique. Know what you want. Then construct a single event, an event which implies fulfillment of your wish. Restrict the event to a single act.

For instance, if I single out as an event, shaking a man's hand, then that is the only thing I do. I do not shake it, then light a cigarette and do a thousand other things. I simply imagine that I am actually shaking hands and keep the act going over and over and over again until the imaginary act has all the feeling of reality.

The event must always imply fulfillment of the wish. Always construct an event which you believe you would naturally encounter following the fulfillment of your desire. You are the judge of what event you really want to realize.

There is another technique I gave you last night. If you cannot concentrate on an act, if you cannot snuggle into your chair and believe the chair is elsewhere, just as though elsewhere were here, then do this: Reduce the idea, condense it to a single, simple phrase like, "Isn't it wonderful." or, "Thank you." or, "It's done." or, "It's finished."

There should not be more than three words. Something that implies the desire is already realized. "Isn't it wonderful", or "Thank you," certainly imply that. These are not all the phrases you could use. Make up out of your own vocabulary the phrase which best suits you. But make it very, very short and always use a phrase that implies fulfillment of the idea.

When you have your phrase in mind, lift the cloud. Let the cloud ascend by simply inducing the state that borders on sleep. Simply begin to imagine and feel you are sleepy, and in this state assume the feeling of the wish fulfilled. Then repeat the phrase over and over like a lullaby. Whatever the phrase is, let it imply that the assumption is true, that it is concrete, that it is already a fact and you know it.

Just relax and enter into the feeling of actually being what you want to be. As you do it you are entering Jericho with your spy who has the power to give it. You are releasing Barabbas and sentencing Jesus to be crucified and resurrected. All these stories you are re-enacting if now you begin to let go and enter into the feeling of actually being what you want to be. Now we can go. . . .

SILENCE PERIOD.

If your hands are dry, and if your mouth is dry at the end of this meditation, that is positive proof that you did succeed in lifting the cloud. What you were doing when the cloud was lifted is entirely your business. But you did lift the cloud if your hands are dry.

I will give you another phenomena which is very strange and one I cannot analyze. It happens if you really go into the deep. You will find on waking that you have the most active pair of kidneys in the world. I have discussed it with doctors and they cannot explain it.

Another thing you may observe in meditation is a lovely liquid blue light. The nearest thing on earth to which I can compare it is burning alcohol. You know when you put alcohol on the plum pudding at Christmas time and set it aflame, the lovely liquid blue flame that envelopes the pudding until you blow it out. That flame is the nearest thing to the blue light which comes on the forehead of a man in meditation.

Do not be distressed. You will know it when you see it. It is like two shades of blue, a darker and a lighter blue in constant motion, just like burning alcohol, which is unlike the constant flame of a gas jet. This flame is alive, just as spirit would be alive.

Another thing that may come to you as it did to me. You will see spots before your eyes. They are not liver spots as some people will tell you who know nothing about it. These are little things that float in space like a mesh, little circles all tied together. They start with a single cell and come in groups in different geometrical patterns, like worms, like trailers, and they float all over your face. When you close your eyes you still see them, proving that they are not from without, they are from within.

When you begin to expand in consciousness all these things come. They may be your blood stream objectified by some strange trick of man that man does not quite understand. I am not denying that it is your blood stream made visible, but do not be distressed by thinking it is liver spots or some other silly thing that people will tell you.

If these various phenomena come to you, do not think you are doing something wrong. It is the normal, natural expansion that comes to all men who take themselves in tow and try to develop the garden of Gethscmane.

The minute you begin to discipline your mind by observing your thoughts and watching your thoughts throughout the day, you become the policeman of your thoughts. Refuse to enter into conversations that are unlovely, refuse to listen attentively to anything that tears down.

Begin to build within your own mind's eye the vision of the perfect virgin rather than the vision of the foolish virgin. Listen only to the things that bring joy when you hear them. Do not give a willing ear to that which is unlovely, which when you heard it you wish you had not. That is listening and seeing things without oil in your lamp, or joy in your mind.

There are two kinds of virgins in the Bible: five foolish and five wise virgins. The minute you become the wise virgin, or try to make an attempt to do it, you will find all these things happen. You will see these things, and they interest you so that you have not time to develop the foolish sight, as many people do. I hope that no one here does. Because no one should be identified with this great work who can still find great joy in a discussion of another that is unlovely.

Lesson 3

THINKING FOURTH-DIMENSIONALLY

There are two actual outlooks on the world possessed by every man, and the ancient story tellers were fully conscious of these two outlooks. They called the one "the carnal mind," and the other "the mind of Christ."

We recognize these two centers of thought in the statement: "The natural man receiveth not the things of the Spirit of God: for they are foolishness unto him: neither can he know them, because they are spiritually discerned." 1 Cor. 2:14.

To the natural mind, reality is confined to the instant called now; this very moment seems to contain the whole of reality, everything else is unreal. To the natural mind, the past and the future are purely imaginary. In other words my past, when I use the natural mind, is only a memory image of things that were. And to the limited focus of the carnal or natural mind the future does not exist. The natural-mind does not believe that it could revisit the past and see it as something that is present, something that is objective and concrete to itself, neither does it believe that the future exists.

To the Christ mind, the spiritual mind, which in our language we will call the fourth-dimensional focus, the past, the present, and the future of the natural mind are a present whole. It takes in the entire array of sensory impressions that man has encountered, is encountering, and will encounter.

The only reason you and I are functioning as we are today, and are not aware of the greater outlook, is simply because we are creatures of habit, and habit renders us totally blind to what otherwise we should see; but habit is not law. It acts as though it were the most compelling force in the world, yet it is not law.

We can create a new approach to life. If you and I would spend a few minutes every day in withdrawing our attention from the region of sensation and concentrating it on an invisible state and remain faithful to this contemplation, feeling and sensing the reality of an invisible state, we would in time become aware of this greater world, this dimensionally larger world. The state contemplated is now a concrete reality, displaced in time.

Tonight as we turn to our Bible you be the judge as to where you stand in your present unfoldment.

Our first story for tonight is from the 5th chapter of the Gospel of Mark. In this chapter there are three stories told as though they were separate experiences of the dominant characters.

In the first story we are told that Jesus came upon an insane man, a naked man who lived in the cemetery and hid himself behind the tombs. This man appealed to Jesus not to cast out the devils that bedeviled him.

But Jesus said unto him, "Come out of the man, thou unclean spirit." Mark 5:8.

Thus Jesus cast out the devils that they may now destroy themselves, and we find this man, for the first time, clothed and in his right mind and seated at the feet of the Master. We will get the psychological sense of this chapter by changing the name Jesus to that of enlightened reason or fourth-dimensional thinking.

As we progress in this chapter we are told that Jesus now comes upon the High Priest whose name is Jairus, and Jairus the High Priest of the synagogue has a child who is dying. She is 12 years old, and he appeals to Jesus to come and heal the child.

Jesus consents, and as he starts toward the home of the High Priest a woman in the market place touched his garment. "And Jesus, immediately knowing in himself that virtue had gone out of him, turned him about in the press, and said, Who touched my clothes?" Mark 5:30.

The woman who was healed of an issue of blood that she had had for 12 years confessed that she had touched him. "And he said unto her, Daughter, thy faith hath made thee whole; go in peace." Mark 5:34.

As he continues toward the home the High Priest he is told that the child is dead and there is no need to go to resurrect her. She is no longer asleep, but is now dead.

"As soon as Jesus heard the word that was spoken, he saith unto the ruler of the synagogue, Be not afraid, only believe." Mark 5:36.

"And when he was come in, he saith unto them, Why make ye this ado, and weep? The damsel is not dead, but sleepeth." Mark 5:39.

With this the entire crowd mocked and laughed, but Jesus, closing the doors against the mocking crowd, took with him into the household of Jairus, his disciples and the father and mother of the dead child.

They entered into the room where the damsel was lying. "And he took the damsel by the hand, and said unto her, damsel, I say unto thee, arise." Mark 5:41.

"From this deep sleep she awoke and arose and walked, and the High Priest and all the others were astonished. And he changed them straightly that no man should know it; and he commanded that something should be given her to eat." Mark 5:43.

You are this very night, as you are seated here, pictured in this 5th chapter of Mark. A cemetery is for one purpose: it is simply a record of the dead. Are you living in the dead past?

If you are living among the dead, your prejudices, your superstitions, and your false beliefs that you keep alive are the tombstones behind which you hide. If you refuse to let them go you are just as mad as the mad man of the Bible who pleaded with enlightened reason not to cast them out. There is no difference. But enlightened reason is incapable of protecting prejudice and superstition against the inroads of reason.

There is not a man in this world who has a prejudice, regardless of the nature of the prejudice, who can hold it up to the light of reason. Tell me you are against a certain nation, a certain race, a certain "ism," a certain anything—I do not care what it is—you cannot expose that belief of yours to the light of reason and have it live. In order that it may be kept alive in your world you must hide it from reason. You cannot analyze it in the light of reason and have it live. When this fourth-dimensional focus comes and shows you a new approach to life and casts out of your own mind all these things that bedeviled you, you are then cleansed and clothed in your right mind. And you sit at the foot of understanding, called the feet of the Master.

Now clothed and in your right mind you can resurrect the dead. What dead? The child in the story is not a child. The child is your ambition, your desire, the unfulfilled dreams of your heart. This is the child housed within the mind of man. For as I have stated before, the entire drama of the Bible is a psychological one. The Bible has no reference at all to any person who ever existed, or any event that ever occurred upon earth. All the stories of the Bible unfold in the minds of the individual man.

In this story Jesus is the awakened intellect of man. When your mind functions outside of the range of your present senses, when your mind is healed of all the former limitations, then you are no longer the insane man; but you are this presence personified as Jesus, the power that can resurrect the longings of the heart of man.

You are now the woman with the issue of blood. What is this issue of blood? A running womb is not a productive womb. She held it for 12 years, she was incapable of conceiving. She could not give form to her longing because of the running of the issue of blood. You are told her faith closed it. As the womb closes it can give form to the seed or idea.

As your mind is cleansed of your former concept of Self, you assume you are what you want to be, and remaining faithful to this assumption, you give form to your assumption or resurrect your child. You are the woman cleansed of the issue of blood, and you move towards the house of the dead child.

The child or state you desired is now your fixed concept of yourself. But now having assumed that I am what formerly I desired to be, I cannot continue desiring what I am conscious of being. So I do not discuss it. I talk to no one concerning what I am. It is so obvious to me that I am what I wanted to be that I walk as though I were.

Walking as though I am what formerly I wanted to be, my world of limited focus does not see it and thinks I no longer desire it. The child is dead within their world; but I, who know the law, say, "The child is not dead." The damsel is not dead, she but sleepeth. I now awaken her. I, by my assumption, awaken and make visible in my world what I assume, for assumptions if sustained invariably awaken what they affirm.

I close the door. What door? The door of my senses. I simply shut out completely all that my senses reveal. I deny the evidence of my senses. I suspend the limited reason of the natural man and walk in this bold assertion that I am what my senses deny.

With the door of my senses closed, what do I take into that disciplined state? I take no one into that state but the parents of the child and my disciples. I close the door against the mocking, laughing crowd. I no longer look for confirmation. I completely deny the evidence of my senses, which mock my assumption and do not discuss with others whether my assumption is possible or not.

Who are the parents? We have discovered that the father-mother of all creation is man's I AMness. Man's consciousness is God. I am conscious of the state. I am the father-mother of all my ideas and my mind remains faithful to this new concept of self. My mind is disciplined. I take into that state the disciples, and I shut out of that state everything that would deny it.

Now the child, unaided by a man, is resurrected. The condition which I desired and assumed that I had, becomes objectified within my world and bears witness to the power of my assumption.

You be the judge, I cannot judge you. You are either living now in the dead past, or you are living as the woman whose issue of blood has been stanched. Could you actually answer me if I asked you the question:

"Do you believe now that you, without the assistance of another, need only assume that you are what you want to be, to make that assumption real within your world? Or do you believe that you must first fulfill a certain condition imposed upon you by the past, that you must be of a certain order, or a certain something?'

I am not being critical of certain churches or groups, but there are those who believe that anyone outside of their church or group is not yet saved. I was born a Protestant. You talk to a Protestant, there is only one Christian, a Protestant. You talk to a Catholic, why there is nothing in the world that is a Christian but a Catholic. You talk to a Jew, and the Christians are heathens, and the Jews are the chosen. You talk to a Mohammedan, Jews and Christians are the infidels. You talk to someone else and all these are the untouchables. It does not matter to whom you talk, they are always the chosen ones.

If you believe that you must be one of these in order to be saved, you are still an insane man hiding behind these superstitions and these prejudices of the past, and you are begging not to be cleansed.

Some of you say to me, "Do not ask me to give up my belief in Jesus the man, or in Moses the man, or in Peter the man. When you ask me to give up my belief in these characters you are asking too much. Leave me these beliefs because they comfort me. I can believe that they lived upon earth and still follow your psychological interpretation of their stories."

I say, come out of the dead past. Come out of that cemetery and walk, knowing that you and your Father are one, and your Father, who men call GOD, is your own consciousness. That is the only creative law in the world.

Of what are you conscious of being? Although you cannot see your objective with the limited focus of your three-dimensional mind, you are now that which you have assumed you are. Walk in that assumption and remain faithful to it.

Time in this dimension of your being, beats slowly and you may not, even after you objectify your assumption, remember there was a time when this present reality was but an attitude of mind. Because of the slowness of the beat of time here you often fail to see the relationship between your inner nature and the outer world that bears witness to it.

You be the judge of the position you now occupy in this 5th chapter of Mark. Are you resurrecting the dead child? Are you still in need of having that womb of your mind closed? Is it still running and therefore cannot be fertile? Are you now the insane man living in the dead past? Only you can be the judge and answer these questions.

Now we turn to a story in the 5th chapter of the Gospel of John. This will show you how beautifully the ancient-story tellers told of the two distinct outlooks on this world—one, the limited three-dimensional focus, and the other, the fourth-dimensional focus.

This story tells of an impotent man who is quickly healed. Jesus comes to a place called Bethesda, which by definition means the House of Five Porches. On these Five Porches are unnumbered impotent folk— lame, blind, halt, withered, and others. Tradition had it that at certain seasons of the year an angel would descend and disturb the pool which was near these Five Porches. As the Angel disturbed the pool, the first one in was always healed. But only the first one, not the second.

Jesus, seeing a man who was lame from his mother's womb, said to him, "Wilt thou be made whole?" John 5:6.

"The impotent man answered him, Sir, I have no man, when the water is troubled, to put me into the pool—but while I am coming, another steppeth down before me." John 5:7.

"Jesus saith unto him, Rise, take up thy bed, and walk." John 5:8.

"And immediately the man was made whole, and took up his bed, and walked, and on the same day was the Sabbath." John 5:9.

You read this story and you think some strange man who possessed miraculous power suddenly said to the lame man, "Rise and walk." I cannot repeat too often that the story, even when it introduces numberless individualities, takes place within the mind of the individual man.

The pool is your consciousness. The angel is an idea, called the messenger of GOD. Consciousness being God, when you have an idea you are entertaining an angel. The minute you are conscious of a desire your pool has been disturbed. Desire disturbs the mind of man. To want something is to be disturbed.

The very moment you have an ambition, or a clearly defined objective, the pool has been disturbed by the angel, which was the desire. You are told that the first one into the disturbed pool is always healed.

My closest companions in this world, my wife and my little girl, are to me when I address them, second. I must speak to my wife as, "you are." I must speak to anyone, no matter how close they are, as "You are." And after that the third person, "He is." There is only one person in this world with whom I can use the first person present and that is self. "I am," can be said only of myself, it cannot be said of another.

Therefore, when I am conscious of some desire that I want to be, but seemingly am not, the pool being disturbed, who can get into that pool before me? I alone possess the power of the first person. I am that which I want to be. Except I believe I am what I want to be, I remain as I formerly was and die in that limitation.

In this story you need no man to put you into the pool as your consciousness is disturbed by desire. All you need do is to assume you are already that which formerly you wanted to be and you are in it, and no man can get in before you. What man can get in before you when you become conscious of being that which you want to be? No one can be before you when you alone possess the power to say I AM.

These are the two outlooks. You are now what your senses would deny. Are you bold enough to assume that you are already that which you want to be? If you dare assume you are already that which your reason and your senses now deny, then you are in the pool and, unaided by a man, you, too, will rise and take your couch and walk.

You are told it happened on the Sabbath. The Sabbath is only the mystical sense of stillness, when you are unconcerned, when you are not anxious, when you are not looking for results, knowing that signs follow and do not precede.

The Sabbath is the day of stillness wherein there is no working. When you are not working to make it so you are in the Sabbath. When you are not at all concerned about the opinion of others, when you walk as though you were, you cannot raise one finger to make it so, you are in the Sabbath. I cannot be concerned as to how it will be, and still say I am conscious of being it. If I am conscious of being free, secure, healthy, and happy, I sustain these states of consciousness without effort or labor on my part. Therefore, I am in the Sabbath; and because it was the Sabbath he rose and walked.

Our next story is from the 4th chapter of the Gospel of John, and it is one you have heard time and time again. Jesus comes to the well and there is a woman called the woman of Samaria, and he said to her, "Give me to drink." John 4:7.

"Then saith the woman of Samaria unto him, How is it that thou, being a Jew, asketh drink of me, which am a woman of Samaria? For the Jews have no dealings with the Samaritans." John 4:9.

"Jesus answered and said unto her, If thou knewest the gift of God, and who it is that saith to thee, Give me to drink; thou wouldest have asked of him, and he would have given thee living water." John 4:10.

The woman seeing that he has nothing with which to draw the water, and knowing the well is deep, says: "Art thou greater than our father Jacob, which gave us the well, and drank thereof himself, and his children, and his cattle?" John 4:12.

Jesus answered and said unto her, "Whosoever drinketh of this water shall thirst again. But whosoever drinketh of the water that I shall give him shall never thirst; but the water that I shall give him shall be in him a well of water springing up into everlasting life." John 4:13,14.

Then he tells her all concerning herself and asks her to go and call her husband. She answered and said, "I have no husband." John 4:17.

"Jesus said unto her, Thou hast well said, I have no husband: For thou hast had five husbands; and he whom thou now hast is not thy husband." John 4:17, 18.

The woman, knowing this to be true, goes into the marketplace and tells the other, "I have met the Messiah."

They ask her, "How do you know you have met the Messiah?"

"Because he told me all things that I have ever done," she replies. Here is a focus that takes in the entire past at least, and tells her now concerning the future.

Continuing with the story, the disciples come to Jesus and say, "Master, eat." John 4:31.

"But he said unto them, I have meat to eat that ye know not of." John 4:32.

When they speak of a harvest in four months, Jesus replies, "Say not ye, There are yet four months, and then cometh harvest? Behold, I say unto you, lift up your eyes, and look on the fields; for they are white already to harvest." John 4:35.

He sees things that people wait four months for, or wait four years for; he sees them as now in a dimensionally larger world, existing now, taking place now.

Let us go back to the first part of the story. The woman of Samaria is the three-dimensional you, and Jesus at the well is the fourth-dimensional you. The argument starts between what you want to be, and what reason tells you that you are. The greater you tells you that if you would dare assume you are already what you want to be, you would become it.

The lesser you, with its limited focus, tells you, "Why you haven't a bucket, you haven't a rope and the well is deep. How could you ever reach the depth of this state without the means to that end?"

You answer and say, "If you only knew who asks of you to drink you would ask of him." If you only knew what in yourself is urging upon you the embodiment of the state you now seek, you would suspend your little sight and let him do it for you.

Then he tells you that you have five husbands, and you deny it. But he knows far better than you that your five senses impregnate you morning, noon, and night with their limitations. They tell you what children you will bear tonight, tomorrow, and the days to come. For your five senses act like five husbands who constantly impregnate your consciousness, which is the great womb of GOD; and morning, noon, and night they suggest to you, and dictate to you that which you must accept as true.

He tells you the one you would like to have for your husband is not your husband. In other words the sixth has not yet impregnated you. What you would like to be is denied by these five, and they hold the power, they dictate what you will accept as true. What you would like to accept has not yet penetrated your mind and impregnated your mind with its reality. He whom you call husband is really not your husband. You are not bearing his likeness. To bear his likeness is proof that you are his wife, at least you have known him intimately. You are not bearing the likeness of the sixth; you are only bearing the likeness of the five.

Then one turns to me and tells me all that I have ever known. I go back in my mind's eye and reason tells me that all through my life I have always accepted the limitations of my senses, I have always looked upon them as fact; and morning, noon, and night I have born witness to this acceptance.

Reason tells me I have only known these five from the time I was born. Now I would like to step outside the limitation of my senses but I have not yet found within myself the courage to assume I am what these five would deny that I am. So here I remain, conscious of my task, but without the courage to step beyond the limitations of my senses, and that which my reason denies.

He tells these, "I have meat ye know not of. I am the bread that droppeth down from heaven. I am the wine." I know what I want to be, and because I am that bread I feast upon it. I assume that I am, and instead of feasting upon the fact that I am in this room talking to you and you are listening to me, and that I am in Los Angeles, I feast upon the fact that I am elsewhere and I walk here as though I were elsewhere. And gradually I become what I feast upon.

Let me give you two personal stories. When I was a boy I lived in a very limited environment, in a little island called Barbados. Feed for animals was very, very scarce and very expensive because we had to import it. I am one of a family of 10 children and my grandmother lived with us making 13 at the table.

Time and again I can remember my mother saying to the cook in the early part of the week, "I want you to put away three ducks for Sunday's dinner. "This meant that she would take from the flock in the yard three ducks and coop them up in a very small cage and feed them, stuff them morning, noon, and night with corn and all the things she wanted the ducks to feast upon.

This was an entirely different diet from what we regularly fed the ducks, because we kept those birds alive by feeding them fish. We kept them alive and fat on fish because fish were very cheap and plentiful; but you could not eat a bird that fed upon fish, not as you and I like a bird.

The cook would take three ducks, put them in a cage and for seven days stuff them with corn, sour milk and all the things we wanted to taste in the birds. Then when they were killed and served for dinner seven days later they were luscious, milk fed, corn fed birds.

But occasionally the cook forgot to put away the birds, and my father, knowing we were having ducks, and believing that she had carried out the command, did not send anything else for dinner, and three fish came to the table. You could not touch those birds for they were so much the embodiment of what they fed upon.

Man is a psychological being, a thinker. It is not what he feeds upon physically, but what he feeds upon mentally that he becomes. We become the embodiment of that which we mentally feed upon.

Now those ducks could not be fed corn in the morning and fish in the afternoon and something else at night. It had to be a complete change of diet. In our case we cannot have a little bit of meditation in the morning, curse at noon, and do something else in the evening. We have to go on a mental diet, for a week we must completely change our mental food.

"Whatsoever things are true, whatsoever things are honest, whatsoever things are just, whatsoever things are pure, whatsoever things are of good report; if there be any virtue, and if there be any praise, think on these things." Phil. 4:8.

As a man thinketh in his heart so is he. If I could now single out the kind of mental food I want to express within my world and feast upon it, I would become it.

Let me tell you why I am doing what I am doing today. It was back in 1933 in the city of New York, and my old friend Abdullah, with whom I studied Hebrew for five years, was really the beginning of the eating of all my superstitions. When I went to him I was filled with superstitions. I could not eat meat, I could not eat fish, I could not eat chicken, I could not eat any of these things that were living in the world. I did not drink, I did not smoke, and I was making a tremendous effort to live a celibate life.

Abdullah said to me, "I am not going to tell you 'you are crazy' Neville, but you are you know. All these things are stupid." But I could not believe they were stupid.

In November, 1933, I bade goodbye to my parents in the city of New York as they sailed for Barbados. I had been in this country 12 years with no desire to see Barbados. I was not successful and I was ashamed to go home to successful members of my family. After 12 years in America I was a failure in my own eyes. I was in the theatre and made money one year and spent it the next month. I was not what I would call by their standards nor by mine a successful person.

Mind you when I said goodbye to my parents in November I had no desire to go to Barbados. The ship pulled out, and as I came up the street, something possessed me with a desire to go to Barbados.

It was the year 1933, I was unemployed and had no place to go except a little room on 75th Street. I went straight to my old friend Abdullah and said to him "Ab, the strangest feeling is possessing me. For the first time in 12 years I want to go to Barbados." "If you want to go Neville, you have gone." he replied.

That was very strange language to me. I am in New York City on 72nd Street and he tells me I have gone to Barbados. I said to him, "What do you mean, I have gone, Abdullah?"

He said, "Do you really want to go?"

I answered, "yes."

He then said to me, "As you walk through this door now you are not walking on 72nd Street, you are walking on palm-lined streets, coconut-lined streets; this is Barbados. Do not ask me how you are going to go. You are in Barbados. You do not say 'how' when you 'are there'. You are there. Now you walk as though you were there."

I went out of his place in a daze. I am in Barbados. I have no money, I have no job, I am not even well clothed, and yet I am in Barbados.

He was not the kind of a person with whom you would argue, not Abdullah. Two weeks later I was no nearer my goal than on the day I first told him I wanted to go to Barbados. I said to him, "Ab, I trust you implicitly but here is one time I cannot see how it is going to work. I have not one penny towards my journey, I began to explain."

You know what he did. He was as black as the ace of spades, my old friend Abdullah, with his turbaned head. As I sat in his living room he rose from his chair and went towards his study and slammed the door, which was not an invitation to follow him. As he went through the door he said to me, "I have said all that I have to say."

On the 3rd of December I stood before Abdullah and told him again I was no nearer my trip. He repeated his statement, "You are in Barbados."

The very last ship sailing for Barbados that would take me there for the reason I wanted to go, which was to be there for Christmas, sailed at noon on December 6th, the old Nerissa.

On the morning of December 4th, having no job, having no place to go, I slept late. When I got up there was an air mail letter from Barbados under my door. As I opened the letter a little piece of paper flickered to the floor. I picked it up and it was a draft for $50.00.

The letter was from my brother Victor and it read, "I am not asking you to come, Neville, this is a command. We have never had a Christmas when all the members of our family were present at the same time. This Christmas it could be done if you would come."

My oldest brother Cecil left home before the youngest was born and then we started to move away from home at different times so never in the history of our family were we ever all together at the same time.

The letter continued, "You are not working, I know there is no reason why you cannot come, so you must be here before Christmas. The enclosed $50.00 is to buy a few shirts or a pair of shoes you may need for the trip. You will not need tips; use the bar if you are drinking. I will meet the ship and pay all your tips and your incurred expenses. I have cabled Furness, Withy & Co. in New York City and told them to issue you a ticket when you appear at their office. The $50.00 is simply to buy some little essentials. You may sign as you want aboard the ship. I will meet it and take care of all obligations."

I went down to Furness, Withy & Co. with my letter and let them read it. They said, "We received the cable Mr. Goddard, but unfortunately we have not any space left on the December 6th sailing. The only thing available is 3rd Class between New York and St. Thomas. When we get to St. Thomas we have a few passengers who are getting off. You may then ride 1st Class from St. Thomas to Barbados. But between New York and St. Thomas you must go 3rd Class, although you may have the privileges of the 1st Class dining room and walk the decks of the 1st Class."

I said, "I will take it."

I went back to my friend Abdullah on the afternoon of December 4th and said, "It worked like a dream." I told him what I had done, thinking he would be happy.

Do you know what he said to me? He said, "Who told you that you are going 3rd Class? Did I see you in

Barbados, the man you are, going 3rd Class? You are in Barbados and you went there 1st Class."

I did not have one moment to see him again before I sailed on the noon of December 6th. When I reached the dock with my passport and my papers to get aboard that ship the agent said to me, "We have good news for you, Mr. Goddard. There has been a cancellation and you are going 1st Class."

Abdullah taught me the importance of remaining faithful to an idea and not compromising. I wavered, but he remained faithful to the assumption that I was in Barbados and had traveled 1st Class.

Now back to the significance of our two Bible stories. The well is deep and you have no bucket, you have no rope. It is four months to the harvest and Jesus says, "I have meat to eat ye know not of. I am the bread of heaven."

Feast on the idea, become identified with the idea as though you were already that embodied state. Walk in the assumption that you are what you want to be. If you feast on that and remain faithful to that mental diet, you will crystallize it. You will become it in this world.

When I came back to New York in 1934, after three heavenly months in Barbados, I drank, I smoked, and did everything I had not done in years.

I remembered what Abdullah had said to me, "After you have proven this law you will become normal, Neville. You will come out of that graveyard, you will come out of that dead past where you think you are being holy. For all you are really doing you know, you are being so good, Neville, you are good for nothing"

I came back walking this earth a completely transformed person. From that day, which was in February 1934, I began to live more and more. I cannot honestly tell you I have always succeeded. My many mistakes in this world, my many failures would convict me if I told you that I have so completely mastered the movements of my attention that I can at all times remain faithful to the idea I want to embody.

But I can say with the ancient teacher, although I seem to have failed in the past, I move on and strive day after day to become that which I want to embody in this world. Suspend judgment, refuse to accept what reason and the senses now dictate, and if you remain faithful to the new diet, you will become the embodiment of the ideal to which you remain faithful.

If there is one place in the world that is unlike my little island of Barbados, it is New York City. In Barbados the tallest building is three stories, and the streets are lined with palm trees and cocoanut trees and all sorts of tropical things. In New York City you must go to a park to find a tree.

Yet I had to walk the streets of New York as though I walked the streets of Barbados. To one's imagination all things are possible. I walked, feeling that I was actually walking the streets of Barbados, and in that assumption I could almost smell the odor of the cocoanut lined lanes. I began to create within my mind's eye the atmosphere I would physically encounter were I in Barbados.

As I remained faithful to this assumption, somebody canceled passage and I received it. My brother in Barbados, who never thought of my coming home, has the commanding urge to write me a strange letter. He had never dictated to me, but this time he dictated, and thought that he originated the idea of my visit.

I went home and had three heavenly months, returned 1st Class, and brought back quite a sum of cash in my pocket, a gift. My trip, had I paid for it, would have been $3,000, yet I did it without a nickel in my pocket.

"I have ways ye know not of. My ways are past finding out." The dimensionally greater self took my assumption as the command and influenced the behaviour of my brother to write that letter, influenced the behaviour of someone to cancel that 1st Class passage, and did all the things necessary that would tend toward the production of the idea with which I was identified.

I was identified with the feeling of being there. I slept as though I were there, and the entire behaviour of man was molded in harmony with my assumption. I did not need to go down to Furness, Withy & Co. and beg them for a passage, asking them to cancel some one who was booked 1st Class. I did not need to write my brother and beg him to send me some money or buy me a passage. He thought he originated the act. Actually, to this day, he believes that be initiated the desire to bring me home.

My old friend Abdullah simply said to me, "You are in Barbados, Neville. You want to be there; wherever you want to be, there you are. Live as though you are and that you shall be."

These are the two outlooks. on the world possessed by every man. I do not care who you are. Every child born of woman, regardless of race, nation, or creed, possesses two distinct outlooks on the world.

You are either the natural man who receiveth not the things of the Spirit of God, because to you in the natural focus they are foolishness unto you. Or you are the spiritual man who perceiveth things outside of the limitations of your senses because all things are now realities in a dimensionally larger world. There is no need to wait four months to harvest.

You are either the woman of Samaria or Jesus at the well. You are the man waiting on the Five Porches for the disturbance and someone to push him in; or you are the one who can command yourself to rise and walk in spite of others who wait.

Are you the man behind the tombstones in the cemetery waiting and begging not to be clean, because you do not want to be cleansed of your prejudices? One of the most difficult things for man to give up is his superstitions, his prejudice. He holds on to these as though they were the treasure of treasures.

When you do become cleansed and you are free, then the womb, your own mind is automatically healed. It becomes the prepared ground where seeds, your desires, can take root and grow into manifestation. The child you now bear in your heart is your present objective. Your present longing is a child that is as though it were sick. If you assume you are now what you would like to be, the child for a moment becomes dead because there is no disturbance any more.

You cannot be disturbed when you feel you are what you want to be because if you feel you are what you wanted to be, you are satisfied in that assumption. To others who judge superficially you seem no longer to desire, so to them the desire or damsel is dead. They think you have lost your ambition because you no longer discuss your secret ambition. You have completely adjusted yourself to the idea. You have assumed that you are what you want to be. You know, "She is not dead, she but sleepth." "I go to awaken her."

I walk in the assumption that I am, and as I walk, I quietly awaken her. Then when she awakens I will do the normal, natural thing, I will give her to eat. I will not brag about it and tell others. I simply go and tell no man. I feed this state I now like with my attention. I keep it alive within my world by becoming attentive to it.

Things that I am not attentive to fade and wither within my world, regardless of what they are. They are not just born and then remain unfed. I gave them birth by reason of the fact that I became conscious of being them. When I embody them within my world that is not the end. That is the beginning. Now I am a mother who must keep alive this state by being attentive to it. The day that I am not attentive, I have withdrawn my milk from it, and it fades from my world, as I become attentive to something else in my world.

You can either be attentive to the limitations and feed these and make them mountains, or you can be attentive to your desires; but to become attentive you must assume you are already that which you wanted to be.

Although today we speak of a third-dimensional and a fourth-dimensional focus, do not think for one moment these ancient teachers were not fully conscious of these two distinct centers of thought within the minds of all men. They personified these two, and they tried to show man that the only thing which robs him of the man he could be, is habit. Although it is not law, every psychologist will tell you that habit is the most inhibiting force in the world. It completely restricts man and binds him and makes him totally blind to what otherwise he should be.

Begin now to mentally see and feel yourself as that which you want to be, and feast upon that sensation morning, noon, and night. I have scoured the Bible for a time interval that is longer than three days and I have not found it.

"Jesus answered and said unto them, Destroy this temple, and in three days I will raise it up." John 2:19.

"Prepare you victuals; for within three days ye shall pass over this Jordan, to go in to possess the land, which the Lord your God giveth you to possess it." Joshua 1:11.

If I could completely saturate my mind with one sensation and walk as though it were already-a-fact, I am promised (and I cannot find any denial of it in this great book) that I do not need more than a three-day diet if I remain faithful to it. But I must be honest about it. If I change my diet in the course of the day, I extend the time interval.

You ask me, "But how do I know about the interval?" You, yourself determine the interval.

We have today in our modern world a little word which confuses most of us. I know it confused me until I dug deeper. The word is "action." Action is supposed to be the most fundamental thing in the world. It is not an atom, it is more fundamental. It is not a part of an atom like an electron, it is more fundamental than that. They call it the fourth-dimensional unit. The most fundamental thing in the world is action.

You ask, "What is action?" Our physicists tell us that it is energy multiplied by time. We become more confused and say, "Energy multiplied by time, what does that mean?," They answer, "There is no response to a stimulus, no matter how intense the stimulus, unless it endures for a certain length of time." There must be a minimum endurance to the stimulus or there is no response. On the other hand there is no response to time unless there is a minimum degree of intensity. Today the most fundamental thing in the world is called action, or simply energy multiplied by time.

The Bible gives it as three days; the duration is three days for response in this world. If I would now assume I am what I want to be, and if I am faithful to it and walk as though I were, the very longest stretch given for its realization is three days.

If there is something tonight that you really want in this world, then experience in imagination what you would experience in the flesh were you to realize your goal and deafen your ears, and blind your eyes to all that denies the reality of your assumption.

If you do this you would be able to tell me before I leave this city of Los Angeles that you have realized what was only a wish when you came here. It will be my joy to rejoice with you in the knowledge that the child which was seemingly dead is now alive. This damsel really was not dead, she was only asleep. You fed her in this silence because you have meat no one else knows of. You gave her food and she became a resurrected living reality within your world. Then you can share your joy with me and I can rejoice in your joy.

The purpose of these lessons is to remind you of the law of your own being, the law of consciousness; you are that law. You were only unconscious of its operation. You fed and kept alive the things you did not wish to express within this world.

Take my challenge and put this philosophy to the test. If it does not work you should not use it as a comforter. If it is not true, you must completely discard it. I know it is true. You will not know it until you try either to prove or disprove it.

Too many of us have joined "isms" and we are afraid to put them to the test because we feel we might fail; and, then, where are we? Not really wanting to know the truth concerning it, we hesitate to be bold enough to put it to the test. You say, "I know it would work in some other way. I do not want to really test it. While I have not yet disproved it, I can still be comforted by it."

Now do not fool yourself, do not think for one second be that you are wise.

Prove or disprove this law. I know that if you attempt to disprove it, you will prove it, and I will be the richer for your proving it, not in dollars, not in things, but because you become the living fruit of what I believe I am teaching in this world. It is far better to have you a successful, satisfied person after five days of instruction than to have you go out dissatisfied. I hope you will be bold enough to challenge this instruction and either prove or disprove it.

Now before we go into the silence period I shall briefly explain the technique again. We have two techniques in applying this law. Everyone here must now know exactly what he wants. You must know that if you do not get it tonight you will still be as desirous tomorrow concerning this objective.

When you know exactly what you want, construct in your mind s eye a single, simple event which implies

fulfillment of your desire, an event where in self predominates. Instead of sitting back and looking at yourself as though you were on the screen, you be the actor
in the drama.

Restrict the event to one single action. If you are
going to shake a hand because that implies fulfillment
of your desire then do that and that only. Do not shake
hands and then wander off in your imagination to a
dinner party or to some other place. Restrict your action
to simply shaking hands and do it over and over again,
until that handshake takes on the solidity and the distinctness of reality.

If you feel you cannot remain faithful to an action,
I want you now to define your objective, and then condense the idea, which is your desire, into a single phrase,
a phrase which implies fulfillment of your desire, some
phrase such as, "Isn't it wonderful?"

Or if I felt thankful because I thought someone was
instrumental in bringing my desire to pass, I could say,
"Thank you," and repeat it with feeling over and over
again like a lullaby until my mind was dominated by the
single sensation of thankfulness.

We will now sit quietly in these chairs with the idea
which implies fulfillment of our desire condensed to a
single phrase, or to a single act. We will relax and immobilize our physical bodies. Then let us experience in

imagination the sensation which our condensed phrase or action affirms.

If you imagine yourself shaking another person's hand, do not use your physical hand, let it remain immobilized. But imagine that housed within your hand is a more subtle, more real hand, which can be extracted in your imagination. Put your imaginary hand into the imaginary hand of your friend who stands before you and feel the handshake. Keep your physical body immobilized even though you become mentally active in what you are now about to do.

Now we will go into the silence.

NO ONE TO CHANGE BUT SELF

May I take just a minute to clarify what was said last night. A lady felt from what I said last night that I am anti one nation. I do hope that I am not anti any nation, race or belief. If perchance I used a nation, it was only to illustrate a point.

What I tried to tell you was this—we become what we contemplate. For it is the nature of love, as it is the nature of hate, to change us into the likeness of that which we contemplate. Last night I simply read a news item to show you that when we think we can destroy our image by breaking the mirror, we are only fooling ourselves.

When, through war or revolution, we destroy titles which to us represent arrogance and greed, we become in time the embodiment of that which we thought we had destroyed. So today the people who thought they destroyed the tyrants are themselves that which they thought they had destroyed.

That I may not be misunderstood, let me again lay the foundation of this principle. Consciousness is the one and only reality. We are incapable of seeing other than the contents of our own consciousness

Therefore, hate betrays us in the hour of victory and condemns us to be that which we condemn. All conquest results in an exchange of characteristics, so that conquerors become like the conquered foe. We hate others for the evil which is in ourselves. Races, nations, and religious groups have lived for centuries in intimate hostility, and it is the nature of hatred, as it is the nature of love, to change us into the likeness of that which we contemplate.

Nations act toward other nations as their own citizens act toward each other. When slavery exists in a state and that nation attacks another it is with intent to enslave. When there is a fierce economic competition between citizen and citizen, then in war with another nation the object of the war is to destroy the trade of the enemy. Wars of domination are brought about by the will of those who within a state are dominant over the fortunes of the rest.

We radiate the world that surrounds us by the intensity of our imagination and feeling. But in this third-dimensional world of ours time beats slowly. And so we do not always observe the relationship of the visible world to our inner nature.

Now that is really what I meant. I thought I had said it. That I may not be misunderstood, that is my principle. You and I can contemplate an ideal, and become it by falling in love with it.

On the other hand we can contemplate something we heartily dislike and by condemning it we will become it. But because of the slowness of time in this three-dimensional world, when we do become what we contemplated we have forgotten that formerly we set out to worship or destroy it.

Tonight's lesson is the capstone of the Bible, so do give me your attention. The most important question asked in the Bible will be found in the 16th chapter of the Gospel of St. Matthew.

As you know, all of the Bible stories are your stories; its characters live only in the mind of man. They have no reference at all to any person, who lived in time and space, or to any event that ever occurred upon earth.

The drama related in Matthew takes place in this manner Jesus turns to his disciples and asks them, "Whom do men say that I the Son of man am?" Matt. 16:13.

"And they said, Some say that thou art John the Baptist: some, Elias; and others, Jeremiah, or one of the prophets."

"He saith unto them, But whom say ye that I am?"

"And Simon Peter answered and said, Thou are the Christ, the Son of the living God."

"And Jesus answered and said unto him, Blessed art thou, Simon Bar-Jonah: for flesh and blood hath not revealed it unto thee, but my Father which is in heaven."

"And I say also unto thee that thou art Peter, and upon this rock I will build my church." Matt. 16:14–18.

Jesus turning to his disciples is man turning to his disciplined mind in self-contemplation. You ask yourself the question, "Whom do men say that I am?" In our language, "I wonder what men think of me?"

You answer, "Some say John come again, Some say Elias, others say Jeremiah, and still others a Prophet of old come again."

It is very flattering to be told that you are, or that you resemble, the great men of the past, but enlightened reason is not enslaved by public opinion. It is only concerned with the truth so it asks itself another question, "But whom say ye that I am?" In other words, "Who am I?"

If I am bold enough to assume that I am Christ Jesus, the answer will come back, "Thou are Christ Jesus."

When I can assume it and feel it and boldly live it, I will say to myself, "Flesh and blood could not have told me this. But my Father which is in Heaven revealed it unto me." Then I make this concept of Self the rock on which I establish my church, my world.

"If ye believe not that I am He, ye shall die in your sins." John 8:24.

Because consciousness is the only reality I must assume that I am already that which I desire to be. If I do not believe that I am already what I want to be, then I remain as I am and die in this limitation.

Man is always looking for some prop on which to lean. He is always looking for some excuse to justify failure. This revelation gives man no excuse for failure. His concept of himself is the cause of all the circumstances of his life. All changes must first come from within himself; and if he does not change on the outside it is because he has not changed within. But man does not like to feel that he is solely responsible for the conditions of his life.

"From that time many of his disciples went back, and walked no more with him."

"Then said Jesus unto the twelve, Will ye also go away?"

"Then Simon Peter answered him, Lord, to whom shall we go? Thou hast the words of eternal life." John 6:66–68.

I may not like what I have just heard, that I must turn to my own consciousness as to the only reality, the only foundation on which all phenomena can be explained. It was easier living when I could blame another. It was much easier living when I could blame society for my ills, or point a finger across the sea. and blame another nation. It was easier living when I could blame the weather for the way I feel.

But to tell me that I am the cause of all that happens to me that I am forever molding my world in harmony with my inner nature, that is more than man is willing to accept. If this is true, to whom would I go? If these are the words of eternal life, I must return to them, even though they seem so difficult to digest.

When man fully understands this, he knows that public opinion does not matter, for men only tell him who he is. The behaviour of men constantly tell me who I have conceived myself to be.

If I accept this challenge and begin to live by it, I finally reach the point that is called the great prayer of the Bible. It is related in the 17th chapter of the Gospel of St. John, "I have finished the work which thou gavest me to do." John 17:4.

"And now, O Father, glorify thou me with thine own self with the glory which I had with thee before the world was." John 17:5.

"While I was with them in the world, I kept them in thy name: those that thou gavest me I have kept, and none of them is lost, but the son of perdition." John 17:12.

It is impossible for anything to be lost. In this divine economy nothing can be lost, it cannot even pass away. The little flower which has bloomed once, blooms forever. It is invisible to you here with your limited focus, but it blooms forever in the larger dimension of your being, and tomorrow you will encounter it.

All that thou gavest me I have kept in thy name, and none have I lost save the son of perdition. The son of perdition means simply the belief in loss. Son is a concept, an idea. Perdido is loss. I have only truly lost the concept of loss, for nothing can be lost.

I can descend from the sphere where the thing itself now lives, and as I descend in consciousness to a lower level within myself it passes from my world. I say, "I have lost my health. I have lost my wealth. I have lost my standing in the community. I have lost faith. I have lost a thousand things." But the things in themselves, having once been real in my world, can never cease to be. They never become unreal with the passage of time.

I, by my descent in consciousness to a lower level, cause these things to disappear from my sight and I say,

"They have gone; they are finished as far as my world goes." All I need do is to ascend to the level where they are eternal, and they once more objectify themselves and appear as realities within my world.

The crux of the whole 17th chapter of the Gospel of St. John is found in the 19th verse, "And for their sake I sanctify myself, that they also might be sanctified through the truth."

Heretofore I thought I could change others through effort. Now I know I cannot change another unless I first change myself. To change another within my world I must first change my concept of that other; and to do it best I change my concept of self. For it was the concept I held of self that made me see others as I did.

Had I a noble, dignified concept of myself, I never could have seen the unlovely in others.

Instead of trying to change others through argument and force, let me but ascend in consciousness to a higher level and I will automatically change others by changing self. There is no one to change but self; that self is simply your awareness, your consciousness and the world in which it lives is determined by the concept you hold of self. It is to consciousness that we must turn as to the only reality. For there is no clear conception of the origin of phenomena except that consciousness is all and all is consciousness.

You need no helper to bring you what you seek. Do not for one second believe that I am advocating escape from reality when I ask you to simply assume you are now the man or the lady that you want to be.

If you and I could feel what it would be like were we now that which we want to be, and live in this mental atmosphere as though it were real, then, in a way we do not know, our assumption would harden into fact. This is all we need do in order to ascend to the level where our assumption is already an objective, concrete reality.

I need change no man, I sanctify myself and in so doing I sanctify others. To the pure all things are pure. "There is nothing unclean of itself: but to him that esteemeth anything to be unclean, to him it is unclean." Rom. 14:14. There is nothing in itself unclean, but you, by your concept of self, see things either clean or unclean.

"I and my Father are one." John 10:30.

"If I do not the works of my Father, believe me not. But if I do, though ye believe not me, believe the works: that ye may know, and believe, that the Father is in me, and I in him." John 10:37, 38.

He made himself one with God and thought it not strange or robbery to do the works of God. You always bear fruit in harmony with what you are. It is the most natural thing in the world for a pear tree to bear pears, an apple tree to bear apples, and for man to mold the circumstances of his life in harmony with his inner nature.

"I am the vine, ye are the branches." John 15:5. A branch has no life save it be rooted in the vine. All I need do to change the fruit is to change the vine.

You have no life in my world save that I am conscious of you. You are rooted in me and, like fruit, you bear witness of the vine that I am. There is no reality in the world other than your consciousness. Although you may now seem to be what you do not want to be, all you need do to change it, and to prove the change by circumstances in your world, is to quietly assume that you are that which you now want to be, and in a way you do not know you will become it.

There is no other way to change this world. "I am the way." My I AMness, my consciousness is the way by which I change my world. As I change my concept of self, I change my world. When men and women help or hinder us, they only play the part that we, by our concept of self, wrote for them, and they play it automatically. They must play the parts they are playing because we are what we are.

You will change the world only when you become the embodiment of that which you want the world to be. You have but one gift in this world that is truly yours to give and that is yourself. Unless you yourself are that which you want the world to be, you will never see it in this world. "Except ye believe not that I am he, ye shall die in your sins." John 8:24.

Do you know that no two in this room live in the same world. We are going home to different worlds tonight. We close our doors on entirely different worlds. We rise tomorrow and go to work, where we meet each other and meet others, but we live in different mental worlds, different physical worlds.

I can only give what I am, I have no other gift to give. If I want the world to be perfect, and who does not, I have failed only because I did not know that I could never see it perfect until I myself become perfect. If I am not perfect I cannot see perfection, but the day that I become it, I beautify my world because I see it through my own eyes. "Unto the pure all things are pure." Titus 1:15.

No two here can tell me that you have heard the same message any one night. The one thing that you must do is hear what I say through that which you are. It must be filtered through your prejudices, your superstitions, and your concept of self. Whatever you are, it must come through that, and be colored by what you are.

If you are disturbed and you would like me to be something other than what I appear to be, then you must be that which you want me to be. We must become the thing that we want others to be or we will never see them be it.

Your consciousness, my consciousness, is the only true foundation in the world. This is that which is called Peter in the Bible, not a man, this faithfulness that cannot turn to anyone, that cannot be flattered when you are told by men you are John come again. That is very flattering to be told you are John the Baptist come again, or the great Prophet Elias, or Jeremiah.

Then I deafen my ears to this very flattering little bit of news men would give me and I ask myself, "But honestly who am I?"

If I can deny the limitations of my birth, my environment, and the belief that I am but an extension of my family tree, and feel within myself that I am Christ, and sustain this assumption until it takes a central place and forms the habitual center of my energy, I will do the works attributed to Jesus. Without thought or effort I will mold a world in harmony with that perfection which I have assumed and feel springing within me.

When I open the eyes of the blind, unstop the ears of the deaf, give joy for mourning and beauty for ashes, then and only then, have I truly established this vine deep within. That is what I would automatically do were I truly conscious of being Christ. It is said of this presence, He proved that He was Christ by His works.

Our ordinary alterations of consciousness, as we pass from one state to another, are not transformations, because each of them is so rapidly succeeded by another in the reverse direction; but whenever our assumption grows so stable as to definitely expel its rivals, then that central habitual concept defines our character and is a true transformation.

Jesus, or enlightened reason, saw nothing unclean in the woman taken in adultery. He said to her, "Hath no man condemned thee?" John 8:10.

"She said, No man, Lord. And Jesus said unto her, neither do I condemn thee; go, and sin no more." John 8:11.

No matter what is brought before the presence of beauty, it sees only beauty. Jesus was so completely identified with the lovely that He was incapable of seeing the unlovely.

When you and I really become conscious of being Christ, we too will straighten the arms of the withered, and resurrect the dead hopes of men. We will do all the things that we could not do when we felt ourselves limited by our family tree. It is a bold step and should not be taken lightly, because to do it is to die. John, the man of three dimensions is beheaded, or loses his three-dimensional focus that Jesus, the fourth-dimensional Self may live.

Any enlargement of our concept of Self involves a somewhat painful parting with strongly rooted hereditary conceptions. The ligaments are strong that hold us in the womb of conventional limitations. All that you formerly believed, you no longer believe. You know now that there is no power outside of your own consciousness. Therefore you cannot turn to anyone outside of self.

You have no ears for the suggestion that something else has power in it. You know the only reality is God, and God is your own consciousness. There is no other God. Therefore on this rock you build the everlasting church and boldly assume you are this Divine Being, self-begotten because you dared to appropriate that which was not given to you in your cradle, a concept of Self not formed in your mother's womb, a concept of self conceived outside of the offices of man.

The story is beautifully told us in the Bible using the two sons of Abraham: one the blessed, Isaac, born outside of the offices of man and the other, Ishmael, born in bondage.

Sarah was much too old to beget a child, so her husband Abraham went in unto the bondservant Hagar, the pilgrim, and she conceived of the old man and bore him a son called Ishmael. Ishmael's hand was against every man and every man's hand against him.

Every child born of woman is born into bondage, born into all that his environment represents, regardless of whether it be the throne of England, the White House, or any great place in the world. Every child born of woman is personified as this Ishmael, the child of Hagar.

But asleep in every child is the blessed Isaac, who is born outside of the offices of man, and is born through faith alone. This second child has no earthly father. He is Self-begotten.

What is the second birth? I find myself man, I cannot go back into my mother's womb, and yet I must be born a second time. "Except a man be born again he cannot enter the kingdom of God." John 3:3.

I quietly appropriate that which no man can give me, no woman can give me. I dare to assume that I am God. This must be of faith, this must be of promise. Then I become the blessed, I become Isaac.

As I begin to do the things that only this presence could do, I know that I am born out of the limitations of Ishmael, and I have become heir to the kingdom. Ishmael could not inherit anything, although his father was Abraham, or God. Ishmael did not have both parents of the godly; his mother was Hagar the bond-woman, and so he could not partake of his father's estate.

You are Abraham and Sarah, and contained within your own consciousness there is one waiting for recognition. In the Old Testament it is called Isaac, and in the New Testament it is called Jesus, and it is born without the aid of man.

No man can tell you that you are Christ Jesus, no man can tell you and convince you that you are God. You must toy with the idea and wonder what it would be like to be God.

No clear conception of the origin of phenomena is possible except that consciousness is all and all is consciousness. Nothing can be evolved from man that was not potentially involved in his nature. The ideal we serve and hope to attain could never be evolved from us were it not potentially involved in our nature.

Let me now retell and emphasize an experience of mine printed by me two years ago under the title, THE SEARCH. I think it will help you to understand this law of consciousness, and show you that you have no one to change but self, for you are incapable of seeing other than the contents of your own consciousness.

Once in an idle interval at sea, I meditated on "the perfect state," and wondered what I would be were I of too pure eyes to behold iniquity, if to me all things were pure and were I without condemnation. As I became lost in this fiery brooding, I found myself lifted above the dark environment of the senses. So intense was feeling I felt myself a being of fire dwelling in a body of air. Voices, as from a heavenly chorus, with the exaltation of those who had been conquerors in a conflict with death, were singing, "He is risen—He is risen," and intuitively I knew they meant me.

Then I seemed to be walking in the night. I soon came upon a scene that might have been the ancient Pool of Bethesda for in this place lay a great multitude of impotent folk—blind, halt, withered—waiting not for the moving of the water as of tradition, but waiting for me.

As I came near, without thought or effort on my part, they were one after the other, molded as by the Magician of the Beautiful. Eyes, hands, feet—all missing members—were drawn from some invisible reservoir and molded in harmony with that perfection which I felt springing within me. When all were made perfect the chorus exulted, "It is finished."

I know this vision was the result of my intense meditation upon the idea of perfection, for my meditations invariably bring about union with the state contemplated. I had been so completely absorbed within the idea that for awhile I had become what I contemplated, and the high purpose with which I had for that moment identified myself drew the companionship of high things and fashioned the vision in harmony with my inner nature.

The ideal with which we are united works by association of ideas to awaken a thousand moods to create a drama in keeping with the central idea.

My mystical experiences have convinced me that there is no way to bring about the perfection we seek other than by the transformation of ourselves. As soon as we succeed in transforming ourselves, the world will melt magically before our eyes and reshape itself in harmony with that which our transformation affirms.

We fashion the world that surrounds us by the intensity of our imagination and feeling, and we illuminate or darken our lives by the concepts we hold of ourselves. Nothing is more important to us than our conception of ourselves, and especially is true of our concept of the deep, dimensionally greater One within us.

Those that help or hinder us, whether they know it or not, are the servants of that law which shapes outward circumstances in harmony with our inner nature. It is our conception of ourselves which frees or constrains us, though it may use material agencies to achieve its purpose.

Because life molds the outer world to reflect the inner arrangement of our minds, there is no way of bringing about the outer perfection we seek other than by the transformation of ourselves. No help cometh from without: the hills to which we lift our eyes are those of an inner range.

It is thus to our own consciousness that we must turn as to the only reality, the only foundation on which all phenomena can be explained. We can rely absolutely on the justice of this law to give us only that which is of the nature of ourselves.

To attempt to change the world before we change our concept of ourselves is to struggle against the nature of things. There can be no outer change until there is first an inner change.

As within, so without.

I am not advocating philosophical indifference when I suggest that we should imagine ourselves as already that which we want to be, living in a mental atmosphere of greatness, rather than using physical means and arguments to bring about the desired changes.

Everything we do, unaccompanied by a change of consciousness, is but futile readjustment of surfaces.

However we toil or struggle, we can receive no more than our concepts of Self affirm. To protest against anything which happens to us is to protest against the law of our being and our ruler ship over our own destiny.

The circumstances of my life are too closely related to my conception of myself not to have been formed by my own spirit from some dimensionally larger storehouse of my being. If there is pain to me in these happenings, I should look within myself for the cause, for I am moved here and there and made to live in a world in harmony with my concept of myself.

If we would become as emotionally aroused over our ideals as we become over our dislikes, we would ascend to the plane of our ideal as easily as we now descend to the level of our hates.

Love and hate have a magical transforming power, and we grow through their exercise into the likeness of what we contemplate. By intensity of hatred we create in ourselves the character we imagine in our enemies. Qualities die for want of attention, so the unlovely states might best be rubbed out by imagining "'beauty for ashes and joy for mourning" rather than by direct attacks on the state from which we would be free.

"Whatsoever things are lovely and of good report, think on these things," for we become that with which we are en rapport.

There is nothing to change but our concept of self. As soon as we succeed in transforming self, our world will dissolve and reshape itself in harmony with that which our change affirms.

I, by descent in consciousness, have brought about the imperfection that I see. In the divine economy nothing is lost. We cannot lose anything save by descent in consciousness from the sphere where the thing has its natural life.

"And now, O Fauber, glorify thou me with thine own self with the glory which I had with thee before the world was." John 17:5.

As I ascend in consciousness the power and the glory that was mine return to me and I too will say "I have finished the work thou gavest me to do." The work is to return from my descent in consciousness, from the level wherein I believed that I was a son of man, to the sphere where I know that I am one with my Father and my Father is God.

I know beyond all doubt that there is nothing for man to do but to change his own concept of himself to assume greatness and sustain this assumption. If we walk as though we were already the ideal we serve, we will rise to the level of our assumption, and find a world in harmony with our assumption. We will not have to lift a finger to make it so, for it is already so. It was always so.

You and I have descended in consciousness to the level where we now find ourselves and we see imperfection because we have descended! When we begin to ascend while here in this three-dimensional world, we find that we move in an entirely different environment, we have entirely different circles of friends, and an entirely different world while still living here. We know the great mystery of the statement, "I am in the world but not of it."

Instead of changing things I would suggest to all to identify themselves with the ideal they contemplate. What would the feeling be like were you of too pure eyes to behold iniquity, if to you all things were pure and you were without condemnation? Contemplate the ideal state and identify yourself with it and you will ascend to the sphere where you as Christ have your natural life.

You are still in that state where you were before the world was. The only thing that has fallen is your concept of self. You see the broken parts which really are not broken. You are seeing them through distorted eyes, as though you were in one of those peculiar amusement gallery's where a man walks before a mirror and he is elongated, yet he is the same man. Or he looks into another mirror and he is all big and fat. These things are seen today because man is what he is.

Toy with the idea of perfection. Ask no man to help you, but let the prayer of the 17th chapter of the Gospel of St. John be your prayer. Appropriate the state that was yours before the world was.

Know the truth of the statement, "None have I lost save the son of perdition." Nothing is lost in all my holy mountain. The only thing that you lose is the belief in loss or the son of perdition.

"And for their sake I sanctify myself, that they also might be sanctified through the truth." John 17:19.

There is no one to change but self. All you need do to make men and women holy in this world is to make yourself holy. You are incapable of seeing anything that is unlovely when you establish within your own mind's eye the fact that you are lovely.

It is far better to know this than to know anything else in the world. It takes courage, boundless courage, because many this night, after having heard this truth will still be inclined to blame others for their predicament. Man finds it so difficult to turn to himself, to his own consciousness as to the only reality. Listen to these words:

"No man can come to me, except the Father which hath sent me draw him." John 6:44.

"I and my Father are one." John 10:30.

"A man can receive nothing, except it be given him from heaven." John 3:27.

"Therefore doth my Father love me, because I lay down my life, that I might take it again. No man taketh it from me, but I lay it down of myself." John 10:17,18.

"You did not choose me, 1 have chosen you." John 15:16.

My concept of myself molds a world in harmony with itself and draws men to tell me constantly by their behaviour who 1 am.

The most important thing in this world to you is your concept of self. When you dislike your environment, the circumstances of life and the behaviour of men, ask yourself, "Who am 1?" It is your answer to this question that is the cause of your dislikes.

If you do not condemn self there will be no man in your world to condemn you. If you are living in the consciousness of your ideal you will see nothing to condemn. "To the pure all things are pure."

Now 1 would like to spend a little time making as clear as 1 can what 1 personally do when 1 pray, what 1 do when 1 want to bring about changes in my world. You will find it interesting, and you will find that it works. No one here can tell me they cannot do it. It is so very simple all can do it. We are what we imagine we are.

This technique is not difficult to follow, but you must want to do it. You cannot approach it with the attitude of mind "Oh well, I'll try it." You must want to do it, because the mainspring of action is desire.

Desire is the mainspring of all action. Now what do 1 want? 1 must define my objective. For example, suppose

I wanted now to be elsewhere. This very moment I really desire to be elsewhere. I need not go through the door, I need not sit down. I need do nothing but stand just where I am and with my eyes closed, assume that I am actually standing where I desire to be. Then I remain in this state until it has the feeling of reality. Were I now elsewhere I could not see the world as I now see it from here. The world changes in its relationship to me as I change my position in space.

So I stand right here, close my eyes, and imagine I am seeing what I would see were I there. I remain in it long enough to feel it to be real. I cannot touch the walls of this room from here, but when you close your eyes and become still you can imagine and feel that you touch it. You can stand where you are and imagine you are putting your hand on that wall. To prove you really are, put it there and slide it up and feel the wood. You can imagine you are doing it without getting off your seat. You can do it and you will actually feel it if you become still enough and intense enough

I stand where I am and I allow the world that I want to see and to enter physically to come before me as though I were there now. In other words, I bring else-where here by assuming that I am there.

Is that clear? I let it come up, I do not make it come up. I simply imagine I am there and then let it happen.

If I want a physical presence, I imagine he is standing here, and I touch him All through the Bible I find these suggestions, "He placed his hands upon them. He touched them."

If you want to comfort someone, what is the automatic feeling? To put your hand on them, you cannot resist it. You meet a friend and the hand goes out automatically, you either shake hands or put your hand on his shoulder.

Suppose you were now to meet a friend that you have not seen for a year and he is a friend of whom you are very fond. What would you do? You would embrace him, wouldn't you? Or you would put your hand upon him.

In your imagination bring him close enough to put your hand upon him and feel him to be solidly real. Restrict the action to just that. You will be amazed at what happens. From then on things begin to move. Your dimensionally greater self will inspire, in all, the ideas and actions necessary to bring you into physical contact. It works that way.

Every day I put myself into the drowsy state; it is a very easy thing to do. But habit is a strange thing in man's world. It is not law, but habit acts as though it were the most compelling law in the world. We are creatures of habit.

If you create an interval every day into which you put yourself into the drowsy state, say at 3 o'clock in the afternoon do you know at that moment everyday you will feel drowsy. You try it for one week and see if I am not right.

You sit down for the purpose of creating a state akin to sleep, as though you were sleepy, but do not push the drowsiness too far, just far enough to relax and leave you in control of the direction of your thoughts. You try it for one week, and every day at that hour, no matter what you are doing, you will hardly be able to keep your eyes open. If you know the hour when you will be free you can create it. I would not suggest that you do it lightly, because you will feel very, very sleepy and you may not want to.

I have another way of praying. In this case I always sit down and I find the most comfortable arm chair imaginable, or I lie flat on my back and relax completely. Make yourself comfortable. You must not be in any position where the body is distressed. Always put yourself into a position where you have the greatest ease. That is the first stage.

To know what you want is the start of prayer. Secondly you construct in your mind's eye one single little event which implies that you have realized your desire. I always let my mind roam on many things that could follow the answered prayer and I single out one that is most likely to follow the fulfillment of my desire. One simple little thing like the shaking of a hand, embracing a person, the receiving of a letter, the writing of a check, or whatever would imply the fulfillment of your desire.

After you have decided on the action which implies that your desire has been realized, then sit in your nice comfortable chair or lie flat on your back, close your eyes for the simple reason it helps to induce this state that borders on sleep.

The minute you feel this lovely drowsy state, or the feeling of gathered togetherness, wherein you feel. I could move if I wanted to, but I do not want to, I could open my eyes if I wanted to, but I do not want to. When you get that feeling you can be quite sure that you are in the perfect state to pray successfully.

In this feeling it is easy to touch anything in this world. You take the simple little restricted action which implies fulfillment of your prayer and you feel it or you enact it. Whatever it is, you enter into the action as though you were an actor in the part. You do not sit back and visualize yourself doing it. You do it.

With the body immobilized you imagine that the greater you inside the physical body is coming out of it and that you are actually performing the proposed action. If you are going to walk, you imagine that you are walking. Do not see yourself walk, FEEL that you are walking.

If you are going to climb stairs, FEEL that you are climbing the stairs. Do not visualize yourself doing it, feel yourself doing it. If you are going to shake a man's hand, do not visualize yourself shaking his hand, imagine your friend is standing before you and shake his hand. But leave your physical hands immobilized and imagine that your greater hand, which is your imaginary hand, is actually shaking his hand.

All you need do is to imagine that you are doing it. You are stretched out in time, and what you are doing, which seems to be a controlled day dream, is an actual act in the greater dimension of your being. You are actually encountering an event fourth-dimensionally before you encounter it here in the three-dimensions of space, and you do not have to raise a finger to bring that state to pass.

My third way of praying is simply to feel thankful. If I want something, either for myself or another, I immobilize the physical body, then I produce the state akin to sleep and in that state just feel happy, feel thankful, which thankfulness implies realization of what I want. I assume the feeling of the wish fulfilled and with my mind dominated by this single sensation I go to sleep. I need do nothing to make it so, because it is so. My feeling of the wish fulfilled implies it is done.

All these techniques you can use and change them to fit your temperament. But 1 must emphasize the necessity of inducing the drowsy state where you can become attentive without effort.

A single sensation dominates the mind, if you pray successfully.

What would 1 feel like, now, were 1 what 1 want to be? When 1 know what the feeling would be like 1 then close my eyes and lose myself in that single sensation and my dimensionally greater Self then builds a bridge of incident to lead me from this present moment to the fulfillment of my mood. That is all you need do. But people have a habit of slighting the importance of simple things.

We are creatures of habit and we are slowly learning to relinquish our previous concepts, but the things we formerly lived by still in some way influence our behaviour. Here is a story from the Bible that illustrates my point.

It is recorded that Jesus told his disciples to go to the crossroads and there they would find a colt, a young colt not yet ridden by a man. To bring the colt to him and if any man ask, "Why do you take this colt?" say, "The Lord has need of it."

They went to the crossroads and found the colt and did exactly as they were told. They brought the unbridled ass to Jesus and He rode it triumphantly into Jerusalem.

The story has nothing to do with a man riding on a little colt. You are Jesus of the story. The colt is the mood you are going to assume. That is the living animal not yet ridden by you. What would the feeling be like were you to realize your desire? A new feeling, like a young Colt, is a very difficult thing to ride unless you ride him with a disciplined mind. If I do not remain faithful to the mood the young colt throws me off. Every time you become conscious that you are not faithful to this mood, you have been thrown from the colt.

Discipline your mind that you may remain faithful to a high mood and ride it triumphantly into Jerusalem, which is fulfillment, or the city of peace.

This story precedes the feast of the Passover. If we would pass from our present state into that of our ideal, we must assume that we are already that which we desire to be and remain faithful to our assumption, for we must keep a high mood if we would walk with the highest.

A fixed attitude of mind, a feeling that it is done will make it so. If I walk as though it were, but every once in a while I look to see if it really is, then I fall off my mood or colt.

If I would suspend judgment like Peter I could walk on the water. Peter starts walking on the water, and then he begins to look unto his own understanding and he begins to go down. The voice said, "Look up, Peter." Peter looks up and he rises again and continues walking on the water.

Instead of looking down to see if this thing is really going to harden into fact, you simply know that it is already so, sustain that mood and you will ride the unbridled colt into the city of Jerusalem All of us must learn to ride the animal straight in to Jerusalem unassisted by a man. You do not need another to help you.

The strange thing is that as we keep the high mood and do not fall, others cushion the blows. They spread the palm leaves before me to cushion my journey. I do not have to be concerned. The shocks will be softened as I move into the fulfillment of my desire. My high mood awakens in others the ideas and actions which tend towards the embodiment of my mood. If you walk faithful to a high mood there will be no opposition and no competition.

The test of a teacher, or a teaching, is to be found in the faithfulness of the taught. I am leaving here on Sunday night. Do remain faithful to this instruction. If you look for causes outside the consciousness of man, then I have not convinced you of the reality of consciousness.

If you look for excuses for failure you will always find them, for you find what you seek. If you seek an excuse for failure, you will find it in the stars, in the numbers, in the tea cup, or most any place. The excuse will not be there but you will find it to justify your failure.

Successful business and professional men and women know that this law works. You will not find it in gossip groups, but you will find it in courageous hearts.

Man's eternal journey is for one purpose: to reveal the Father. He comes to make visible his Father. And his Father is made visible in all the lovely things of this world. All the things that are lovely, that are of good report, ride these things, and have no time for the unlovely in this world, regardless of what it is.

Remain faithful to the knowledge that your consciousness, your I AMness, your awareness of being aware of the only reality. It is the rock on which all phenomena can be explained. There is no explanation outside of that. I know of no clear conception of the origin of phenomena save that consciousness is all and all is consciousness.

That which you seek is already housed within you. Were it not now within you eternity could not evolve it.

No time stretch would be long enough to evolve what is not potentially involved in you.

You simply let it into being by assuming that it is already visible in your world, and remaining faithful to your assumption. it will harden into fact. Your Father has unnumbered ways of revealing your assumption. Fix this in your mind and always remember, "An assumption, though false, if sustained will harden into fact."

You and your Father are one and your Father is everything that was, is and will be. Therefore that which you seek you already are, it can never be so far off as even to be near, for nearness implies separation.

The great Pascal said, "You never would have sought me had you not already found me." What you now desire you already have and you seek it only because you have already found it. You found it in the form of desire. It is just as real in the form of desire as it is going to be to your bodily organs.

You are already that which you seek and you have no one to change but Self in order to express it.

Lesson 5

REMAIN FAITHFUL TO YOUR IDEA

Tonight we have the fifth and last lesson in this course. First I shall give you a sort of summary of what has gone before. Then, since so many of you have asked me to elaborate further on Lesson 3, I shall give you a few more ideas on thinking fourth-dimensionally.

I know that when a man sees a thing clearly he can tell it, he can explain it. This past winter in Barbados a fisherman, whose vocabulary would not encompass a thousand words, told me more in five minutes about the behaviour of the dolphin than Shakespeare with his vast vocabulary could have told me, if he did not know the habits of the dolphin.

This fisherman told me how the dolphin loves to play on a piece of drift-wood, and in order to catch him, you throw the wood out and bait him as you would bait children, because he likes to pretend he is getting out of the water. As I said, this man's vocabulary was very limited, but he knew his fish, and he knew the sea. Because he knew his dolphin he could tell me all about their habits and how to catch them.

When you say you know a thing but you cannot explain it, I say you do not know it, for when you really know it you naturally express it.

If I should ask you now to define prayer, and say to you, "How would you, through prayer, go about realizing an objective, any objective?" If you can tell me, then you know it; but if you cannot tell me, then you do not know it. When you see it clearly in the mind's eye the greater you will inspire the words which are necessary to clothe the idea and express it beautifully, and you will express the idea far better than a man with a vast vocabulary who does not see it as clearly as you do.

If you have listened carefully throughout the past four days, you know now that the Bible has no reference at all to any persons that ever existed, or to any events that ever occurred upon earth.

The authors of the Bible were not writing history, they were writing a great drama of the mind which they dressed up in the garb of history, and then adapted it to the limited capacity of the uncritical, unthinking masses.

You know that every story in the Bible is your story, that when the writers introduce dozens of characters in the same story they are trying to present you with different attributes of the mind that you may employ. You saw it as I took perhaps a dozen or more stories and interpreted them for you.

For instance, many people wonder how Jesus, the most gracious, the most loving man in the world, if he be man, could say to his mother, what he is supposed to have said to her as recorded in the second chapter of the Gospel of St. John. Jesus is made to say to his mother, "Woman, what have I to do with thee?" John 2:4.

You and I, who are not yet identified with the ideal we serve, would not make such a statement to our mother. Yet here was the embodiment of love saying to his mother, "Woman, what have I to do with thee?"

You are Jesus, and your mother is your own consciousness. For consciousness is the cause of all, therefore, it is the great father-mother of all phenomena.

You and I are creatures of habit. We get into the habit of accepting as final the evidence of our senses. Wine is needed for the guests and my senses tell me that there is no wine, and I through habit am about to accept this lack as final. When I remember that my consciousness is the one and only reality, therefore if I deny the evidence of my senses and assume the consciousness of having sufficient wine, I have in a sense rebuked my mother or the consciousness which suggested lack; and by assuming the consciousness of having what I desire for my guests, wine is produced in a way we do not know.

I have just read a note here from a dear friend of mine in the audience. Last Sunday he had an appointment at a church for a wedding; the clock told him he was late, everything told him he was late.

He was standing on a street corner waiting for a street car. There was none in sight. He imagined that, instead of being on the street corner, that he was in the church. At that moment a car stopped in front of him. My friend told the driver of his predicament and the driver said to him, "I am not going that way, but I will take you there." My friend got into the car and was at the church in time for the service. That is applying the law correctly, non-acceptance of the suggestion of lateness. Never accept the suggestion of lack.

In this case I say to myself, "What have I to do with thee?" What have I to do with the evidence of my senses? Bring me all the pots and fill them. In other words, I assume that I have wine and all that I desire. Then my dimensionally greater Self inspires in all, the thoughts and the actions which aid the embodiment of my assumption.

It is not a man saying to a mother, "Woman what have I to do with thee?" It is every man who knows this law who will say to himself, when his senses suggest lack, "what have I to do with thee. Get behind me." I will never again listen to a voice like that, because if I do, then I am impregnated by that suggestion and I will bear the fruit of lack.

We turn to another story in the Gospel of St. Mark where Jesus is hungry.

"And seeing a fig tree afar off having leaves, he came, if haply he might find anything thereon: and when he came to it, he found nothing but leaves; for the time of figs was not yet. And Jesus answered and said unto it, No man eat fruit of thee hereafter for ever. And his disciples heard it." Mark 11:13, 14.

"And in the morning, as they passed by, they saw the fig tree dried up from the roots." Mark 11:20.

What tree am I blasting? Not a tree on the outside. It is my own consciousness. "I am the vine." John 15:1. My consciousness, my I AMness is the great tree, and habit once more suggests emptiness, it suggests barrenness, it suggests four months before I can feast. But I cannot wait four months. I give myself this powerful suggestion that never again will I even for a moment relieve that it will take four months to realize my desire. The belief in lack must from this day on be barren and never again reproduce itself in my mind.

It is not a man blasting a tree. Everything in the Bible takes place in the mind of man: the tree, the city, the people, everything. There is not a statement made in the Bible that does not represent some attribute of the human mind. They are all personifications of the mind and not things within the world.

Consciousness is the one and only reality. There is no one to whom we can turn after we discover that our own awareness is God. For God is the cause of all and there is nothing but God. You cannot say that a devil causes some things and God others. Listen to these words.

"Thus saith the Lord to his anointed, to Cyrus, whose right hand I have holden, to subdue nations before him; and I will loose the loins of kings, to open before him the two leaved gates; and the gates shall not be shut. I will go before thee, and make the crooked places straight: I will break in pieces the gates of brass, and cut in sunder the bars of iron. And I will give thee the treasures of darkness, and hidden riches of secret places, that thou mayest know that I, the Lord, which call thee by thy name, am the God of Israel." Isaiah 45:1, 2, 3.

"I form the light, and create darkness: I make peace, and create evil: I the Lord do all these things." Isaiah 45:7.

"I have made the earth, and created man upon it: I, even my hands, have stretched out the heavens, and all their host have I commanded. I have raised him up in righteousness, and I will direct all his ways: he shall build my city, and he shall let go my captives, not for price nor reward, saith the Lord of hosts." Isaiah 45:12, 13.

"I AM the Lord, and there is none else, there is no God beside me." Isaiah 45:5.

Read these words carefully. They are not my words, they are the inspired words of men who discovered that consciousness is the only reality. If I am hurt, I am self hurt. If there is darkness in my world, I created the darkness and the gloom and the depression. If there is light and joy, I created the light and the joy. There is no one but this I AMness that does all.

You cannot find a cause outside of your own consciousness. Your world is a grand mirror constantly telling you who you are. As you meet people, they tell you by their behaviour who you are.

Your prayers will not be less devout because you turn to your own consciousness for help. I do not think that any person in prayer feels more of the joy, the piety, and the feeling of adoration, than I do when I feel thankful, as I assume the feeling of my wish fulfilled, knowing at the same time it is to myself that I turned.

In prayer you are called upon to believe that you possess what your reason and your senses deny. When you pray believe that you have and you shall receive. The Bible states it this way:

"Therefore I say unto you, What things soever ye desire, when ye pray, believe that ye receive them, and ye shall have them. And when ye stand praying, forgive, if ye have ought against any: that your Father also which is in heaven may forgive you your trespasses. But if ye do not forgive, neither will your Father which is in heaven forgive your trespasses." Mark 11:24, 25, 26.

That is what we must do when we pray. If I hold some thing against another, be it a belief of sickness, poverty, or anything else, I must loose it and let it go, not by using words of denial but by believing him to be what he desires to be. In that way I completely forgive him. I changed my concept of him. I had ought against him and I forgave him. Complete forgetfulness is forgiveness. If I do not forget then I have not forgiven.

I only forgive something when I truly forget. I can say to you until the end of time, "I forgive you." But if every time I see you or think of you, I am reminded of what I held against you, I have not forgiven you at all. Forgiveness is complete forgetfulness. You go to a doctor and he gives you something for your sickness. He is trying to take it from you, so he gives you something in place of it.

Give yourself a new concept of self for the old concept. Give up the old concept completely.

A prayer granted implies that something is done in consequence of the prayer which otherwise would not have been done. Therefore, I myself am the spring of action, the directing mind and the one who grants the prayer.

Anyone who prays successfully turns within, and appropriates the state sought. You have no sacrifice to offer. Do not let anyone tell you that you must struggle and suffer. You need not struggle for the realization of your desire. Read what it says in the Bible.

"To what purpose is the multitude of your sacrifices unto me saith the Lord: I am full of the burnt offerings of rams, and the fat of fed beasts; and I delight not in the blood of bullocks, or of lambs, or of he goats."

"When ye come to appear before me, who hath required that at your hand, to tread my courts?"

"Bring no more vain oblations; incense is an abomination unto me; the new moons and Sabbaths, the calling of assemblies, I cannot endure iniquity and solemn assembly."

"Your new moons and your appointed feasts my soul hates: they have become a burden to me, I am weary of bearing them." Isaiah 1:11–14.

"Ye shall have a song as in the night when a holy solemnity is kept; and gladness of heart, as when one goeth with a pipe to come into the mountain of the Lord, to the mighty One of Israel." Isaiah 30:29.

"Sing unto the Lord a new song, and his praise from the end of the earth." Isaiah 42:10.

"Sing, O ye heavens; for the Lord hath done it: shout, ye lower parts of the earth: break forth into singing, ye mountains, O forest, and every tree therein: for the Lord hath redeemed Jacob, and glorified himself in Israel." Isaiah 44:23.

"Therefore the redeemed of the Lord shall return, and come with singing unto Zion; and everlasting joy shall be upon their head. They shall obtain gladness and joy; and sorrow and mourning shall flee away." Isaiah 51:11.

The only acceptable gift is a joyful heart. Come with singing and praise. That is the way to come before the Lord—your own consciousness. Assume the feeling of your wish fulfilled, and you have brought the only acceptable gift. All states of mind other than that of the wish fulfilled are an abomination; they are superstition and mean nothing.

When you come before me, rejoice, because rejoicing implies that something has happened which you desired. Come before me singing, giving praise, and giving thanks, for these states of mind imply acceptance of the state sought. Put yourself in the proper mood and your own consciousness will embody it.

If I could define prayer for anyone and put it just as clearly as I could, I would simply say, "It is the feeling of the wish fulfilled." If you ask, "What do you mean by that?" I would say, "I would feel myself into the situation of the answered prayer and then I would live and act upon that conviction." I would try to sustain it without effort, that is, I would live and act as though it were already a fact, knowing that as I walk in this fixed attitude my assumption will harden into fact.

Time does not permit me to go any further into the argument that the Bible is not history. But if you have listened attentively to my message these past four nights, I do not think you want any more proof that the Bible is not history. Apply what you have heard and you will realize your desires.

"And now I have told you before it come to pass, that, when it is come to pass, ye might believe." John 14:29.

Many persons, myself included, have observed events before they occurred; that is, before they occurred in this world of three dimensions. Since man can observe an event before it occurs in the three dimensions of space, then life on earth proceeds according to plan; and this plan must exist elsewhere in another dimension and is slowly moving through our space.

If the occurring events were not in this world when they were observed, then to be perfectly logical they must have been out of this world. And whatever is THERE to be seen before it occurs HERE must be "pre-determined" from the point of view of man awake in a three-dimensional world. Yet the ancient teachers taught us that we could alter the future, and my own experience confirms the truth of their teaching.

Therefore, my object in giving this course is to indicate possibilities inherent in man, to show that man can alter his: future; but, thus altered, it forms again a deterministic sequence starting from the point of interference—a future that will be consistent with the alteration.

The most remarkable feature of man's future is its flexibility. The future, although prepared in advance in every detail, has several outcomes. We have at every moment of our lives the choice before us which of several futures we will have.

There are two actual outlooks on the world possessed by everyone—a natural focus and a spiritual focus. The ancient teachers called the one "the carnal mind," and the other "the mind of Christ." We may differentiate them as ordinary waking consciousness, governed by our senses, and a controlled imagination, governed by desire.

We recognize these two distinct centers of thought in the statement: "The natural man receiveth not the things of the Spirit of God: for they are foolishness unto him: neither can he know them, because they are spiritually discerned." I Cor. 2:14.

The natural view confines reality to the moment called NOW. To the natural view, the past and future are purely imaginary. The spiritual view on the other hand sees the contents of time. The past and future are a present whole to the spiritual view. What is mental and subjective to the natural man is concrete and objective to the spiritual man.

The habit of seeing only that which our senses permit renders us totally blind to what, otherwise, we could see. To cultivate the faculty of seeing the invisible, we should often deliberately disentangle our minds from the evidence of the senses and focus our attention on an invisible state, mentally feeling it and sensing it until it has all the distinctness of reality.

Earnest, concentrated thought focused in a particular direction shuts out other sensations and causes
them to disappear. We have only to concentrate on the
state desired in order to see it.

The habit of withdrawing attention from the region
of sensation and concentrating it on the invisible devel-
ops our spiritual outlook and enables us to penetrate
beyond the world of sense and to see that which is invisible. "For the invisible things of him from the creation
of the world are clearly seen." Rom. 1:20. This vision is
completely independent of the natural faculties. Open
it and quicken it!

A little practice will convince us that we can, by
controlling our imagination, reshape our future in
harmony with our desire. Desire is the mainspring of
action. We could not move a single finger unless we had
a desire to move it. No matter what we do, we follow
the desire which at the moment dominates our minds.
When we break a habit, our desire to break it is greater
than our desire to continue the habit.

The desires which impel us to action are those
which hold our attention. A desire is but an awareness
of something we lack and need to make our life more
enjoyable. Desires always have some personal gain in
view, the greater the anticipated gain, the more intense
is the desire. There is no absolutely unselfish desire.

Where there is nothing to gain there is no desire, and consequently no action.

The spiritual man speaks to the natural man through the language of desire. The key to progress in life and to the fulfillment of dreams lies in ready obedience to its voice. Unhesitating obedience to its voice is an immediate assumption of the wish fulfilled. To desire a state is to have it. As Pascal has said, "You would not have sought me had you not already found me."

Man, by assuming the feeling of his wish fulfilled, and then living and acting on this conviction, alters the future in harmony with his assumption. Assumptions awaken what they affirm. As soon as man assumes the feeling of his wish fulfilled, his fourth-dimensional Self finds ways for the attainment of this end, discovers methods for its realization.

I know of no clearer definition of the means by which we realize our desires than to EXPERIENCE IN THE IMAGINATION WHAT WE WOULD EXPERIENCE IN THE FLESH WERE WE TO ACHIEVE OUR GOAL. This imaginary experience of the end with acceptance, wills the means. The fourth-dimensional Self then constructs with its larger outlook the means necessary to realize the accepted end.

The undisciplined mind finds it difficult to assume a state which is denied by the senses. But here is a technique that makes it easy to "call things which are not seen as though they were," that is, to encounter an event before it occurs. People have a habit of slighting the importance of simple things. But this simple formula for changing the future was discovered after years of searching and experimenting.

The first step in changing the future is DESIRE, that is, define your objective—know definitely what you want.

Secondly, construct an event which you believe you would encounter FOLLOWING the fulfillment of your desire—an event which implies fulfillment of your desire—something which will have the action of Self predominant.

Thirdly, immobilize the physical body, and induce a condition akin to sleep by imagining that you are sleepy. Lie on a bed, or relax in a chair. Then, with eyelids closed and your attention focused on the action you intend to experience in imagination, mentally feel yourself right into the proposed action; imagining all the while that you are actually performing the action here and. now.

You must always participate in the imaginary action; not merely stand back and look on, but feel that you are actually performing the action so that the imaginary sensation is real to you.

It is important always to remember that the proposed action must be one which FOLLOWS the fulfillment of your desire. Also you must feel yourself into the action until it has all the vividness and distinctness of reality.

For example, suppose you desire promotion in your office. Being congratulated would be an event you would encounter following the fulfillment of your desire. Having selected this action as the one you will experience in imagination, immobilize the physical body; and induce a state akin to sleep, a drowsy state, but one in which you are still able to control the direction of your thoughts, a state in which you are attentive without effort. Then visualize a friend standing before you. Put your imaginary hand into his. Feel it to be solid and real, and carry on an imaginary conversation with him in harmony with the action.

You do not visualize yourself at a distance in point of space and at a distance in point of time being congratulated on your good fortune. Instead, you make elsewhere HERE, and the future NOW. The future event is a reality NOW in a dimensionally larger world and oddly enough, now in a dimensionally larger world is equivalent to HERE in the ordinary three-dimensional space of everyday life.

The difference between FEELING yourself in action, here and now, and visualizing yourself in action, as though you were on a motion-picture screen, is the difference between success and failure. The difference will be appreciated if you will now visualize yourself climbing a ladder. Then, with eyelids closed imagine that a ladder is right in front of you and FEEL yourself actually climbing it.

Desire, physical immobility bordering on sleep, and imaginary action in which Self feelingly predominates HERE AND NOW, are not only important factors in altering the future, but they are also essential conditions in consciously projecting the spiritual Self.

When the physical body is immobilized and we become possessed of the idea to do something—if we imagine that we are doing it HERE AND NOW and keep the imaginary action feelingly going right up until sleep ensues—we are likely to awaken out of the physical body to find ourselves in a dimensionally larger world with a dimensionally larger focus and actually doing what we desired and imagined we were doing in the flesh.

But whether we awaken there or not, we are actually performing the action in the fourth-dimensional world, and will in the future re-enact it here in the third-dimensional world.

Experience has taught me to restrict the imaginary action, to condense the idea which is to be the object of our meditation into a single act, and to re-enact it over and over again until it has the feeling of reality. Otherwise, the attention will wander off along an associational track, and hosts of associated images will be presented to our attention, and in a few seconds they will lead us hundreds of miles away from our objective in point of space, and years away in point of time.

If we decide to climb a particular flight of stairs, because that is the likely event to follow the realization of our desire, then we must restrict the action to climbing that particular flight of stairs. Should the attention wander off, bring it back to its task of climbing that flight of stairs, and keep on doing so until the imaginary action has all the solidity and distinctness of reality. The idea must be maintained in the field of presentation without any sensible effort on our part. We must, with the minimum of effort, permeate the mind with the feeling of the wish fulfilled.

Drowsiness facilitates change because it favours attention without effort, but it must not be pushed to the state of sleep, in which we shall no longer be able to control the movements of our attention, but a moderate degree of drowsiness in which we are still able to direct our thoughts.

A most effective way to embody a desire is to assume the feeling of the wish fulfilled and then, in a relaxed and sleepy state, repeat over and over again like a lullaby, any short phrase which implies fulfillment of your desire, such as, "Thank you, thank you, thank you," until the single sensation of thankfulness dominates the mind. Speak these words as though you addressed a higher power for having done it for you.

If, however, we seek a conscious projection in a dimensionally larger world, then we must keep the action going right up until sleep ensues. Experience in imagination with all the distinctness of reality what would be experienced in the flesh were we to achieve our goal and we shall in time meet it in the flesh as we met it in our imagination.

Feed the mind with premises—that is, assertions presumed to be true, because assumptions, though false, if persisted in until they have the feeling of reality, will harden into fact.

To an assumption, all means which promote its realization are good. It influences the behaviour of all, by inspiring in all the movements, the actions, and the words which tend towards its fulfillment.

To understand how man molds his future in harmony with his assumption—by simply experiencing in his imagination what he would experience in reality were he to realize his goal—we must know what we mean by a dimensionally larger world, for it is to a dimensionally larger world that we go to alter our future.

The observation of an event before it occurs implies that the event is predetermined from the point of view of man in the three-dimensional world. Therefore to change the conditions here in the three dimensions of space we must first change them in the four dimensions of space.

Man does not know exactly what is meant by a dimensionally larger world, and would no doubt deny the existence of a dimensionally larger Self. He is quite familiar with the three dimensions of length, width and height, and he feels that, if there were a fourth-dimension, it should be just as obvious to him as the dimensions of length, width and height.

Now a dimension is not a line. It is any way in which a thing can be measured that is entirely different from all other ways. That is, to measure a solid fourth-dimensionally, we simply measure it in any direction except that of its length, width and height. Now, is there another way of measuring an object other than those of its length, width and height?

Time measures my life without employing the three dimensions of length, width and height. There is no such thing as an instantaneous object. Its appearance and disappearance are measurable. It endures for a definite length of time. We can measure its life span without using the dimensions of length, width and height. Time is definitely a fourth way of measuring an object.

The more dimensions an object has, the more substantial and real it becomes. A straight line, which lies entirely in one dimension, acquires shape, mass and substance by the addition of dimensions. What new quality would time, the fourth dimension give, which would make it just as vastly superior to solids, as solids are to surfaces and surfaces are to lines? Time is a medium for changes in experience, for all changes take time.

The new quality is changeability. Observe that, if we bisect a solid, its cross section will be a surface; by bisecting a surface, we obtain a line, and by bisecting a line, we get a point. This means that a point is but a cross section of a line; which is, in turn, but across section of a surface; which is, in turn, but a cross section of a solid; which is, in turn, if carried to its logical conclusion, but across section of a four-dimensional object.

We cannot avoid the inference that all three-dimensional objects are but cross sections of four-dimensional bodies. Which means: when I meet you, I meet a cross section of the four-dimensional you— the four-dimensional Self that is not seen. To see the four-dimensional Self I must see every cross section or moment of your life from birth to death, and see them all as coexisting.

My focus should take in the entire array of sensory impressions which you have experienced on earth, plus those you might encounter. I should see them, not in the order in which they were experienced by you, but as a present whole. Because CHANGE is the characteristic of the fourth dimension, I should see them in a state of flux—as a living, animated whole.

Now, if we have all this clearly fixed in our minds, what does it mean to us in this three-dimensional world? It means that, if we can move along times length, we can see the future and alter it if we so desire.

This world, which we think so solidly real, is a shadow out of which and beyond which we may at any time pass. It is an abstraction from a more fundamental and dimensionally larger world—a more fundamental world abstracted from a still more fundamental and dimensionally larger world—and so on to infinity. For the absolute is unattainable by any means or analysis, no matter how many dimensions we add to the world.

Man can prove the existence of a dimensionally larger world by simply focusing his attention on an invisible state and imagining that he sees and feels it. If he remains concentrated in this state, his present environment will pass away, and he will awaken in a dimensionally larger world where the object of his con-templation will be seen as a concrete objective reality.

I feel intuitively that, were he to abstract his thoughts from this dimensionally larger world and retreat still farther within his mind, he would again bring about an externalization of time. He would discover that, every time he retreats into his inner mind and brings about an externalization of time, space becomes dimensionally larger. And he would therefore conclude that both time and space are serial, and that the drama of life is but the climbing of a multitudinous dimensional time block.

Scientists will one day explain WHY there is a serial universe. But in practice HOW we use this serial universe to change the future is more important. To change the future, we need only concern ourselves with two worlds in the infinite series; the world we know by reason of our bodily organs, and the world we perceive independently of our bodily organs.

I have stated that man has at every moment of time the choice before him which of several futures he will have. But the question arises: "How is this possible when the experiences of man, awake in the three-dimensional world, are predetermined?" as his observation of an event before it occurs implies.

This ability to change the future will be seen if we liken the experiences of life on earth to this printed page. Man experiences events on earth singly and successively in the same way that you are now experiencing the words of this page.

Imagine that every word on this page represents a single sensory impression. To get the context, to understand my meaning, you focus your vision on the first word in the upper left-hand corner and then move your focus across the page from left to right, letting it fall on the words singly and successively. By the time your eyes reach the last word on this page you have extracted my meaning.

But suppose on looking at the page, with all the printed words thereon equally present, you decided to rearrange them. You could, by rearranging them, tell an entirely different story, in fact you could tell many different stories.

A dream is nothing more than uncontrolled four-dimensional thinking, or the rearrangement of both past and future sensory impressions. Man seldom dreams of events in the order in which he experiences them when awake. He usually dreams of two or more events which are separated in time fused into a single sensory impression; or else he so completely rearranges his single waking sensory impressions that he does not recognize them when he encounters them in his waking state.

For example, I dreamed that I delivered a package to the restaurant in my apartment building. The hostess said to me, "You can't leave that there," whereupon, the elevator operator gave me a few letters and as I thanked him for them he, in turn, thanked me. At this point, the night elevator operator appeared and waved a greeting to me.

The following day, as I left my apartment, I picked up a few letters which had been placed at my door. On my way down I gave the day elevator operator a tip and thanked him for taking care of my mail, whereupon, he thanked me for the tip.

On my return home that day I overheard a doorman say to a delivery man, "You can't leave that there." As I was about to take the elevator up to my apartment, I was attracted by a familiar face in the restaurant, and as I looked in the hostess greeted me with a smile. That night I escorted my dinner guests to the elevator and as I said good-bye to them, the night operator waved good-night to me.

By simply rearranging a few of the single sensory impressions I was destined to encounter, and by fusing two or more of them into single sensory impressions, I constructed a dream which differed quite a bit from my waking experience.

When we have learned to control the movements of our attention in the four-dimensional world, we shall be able to consciously create circumstances in the three-dimensional world. We learn this control through the waking dream, where our attention can be maintained without effort, for attention minus effort is indispensable to changing the future. We can, in a controlled waking dream, consciously construct an event which we desire to experience in the three-dimensional world.

The sensory impressions we use to construct our waking dream are present realities displaced in time or the four-dimensional world. All that we do in constructing the waking dream is to select from the vast array of sensory impressions those, which, when they are properly arranged, imply that we have realized our desire.

With the dream clearly defined we relax in a chair and induce a state of consciousness akin to sleep. A state which, although bordering on sleep, leaves us in conscious control of the movements of our attention. Then we experience in imagination what we would experience in reality were this waking dream an objective fact.

In applying this technique to change the future it is important always to remember that the only thing which occupies the mind during the waking dream is THE WAKING DREAM, the predetermined action and sensation which implies the fulfillment of our desire. How the waking dream becomes physical fact is not our concern. Our acceptance of the waking dream as physical reality wills the means for its fulfillment.

Let me again lay the foundation of prayer, which is nothing more than a controlled waking dream:

1. Define your objective, know definitely what you want.

2. Construct an event which you believe you will encounter FOLLOWING the fulfillment of your desire—something which will have the action of Self predominant—an event which implies the fulfillment of your desire.

3. Immobilize the physical body and induce a state of consciousness akin to sleep. Then, mentally feel yourself right into the proposed action, until the single sensation of fulfillment dominates the mind; imagining all the while that you are actually performing the action HERE AND NOW so that you experience in imagination what you would experience in the flesh were you now to realize your goal. Experience has convinced me that this is the easiest way to achieve our goal.

However, my own many failures would convict me were I to imply that I have completely mastered the movements of my attention. But I can, with the ancient teacher, say:

"This one thing I do, forgetting those things which are behind, and reaching forth unto those things which are before, I press toward the mark for the prize." Phil. 3:13,14.

Again I want to remind you that the responsibility to make what you have done real in this world is not on your shoulders. Do not be concerned with the HOW, you have assumed that it is done, the assumption has its own way of objectifying itself. All responsibility to make it so is removed from you.

There is a little statement in the book of Exodus which bears this out. Millions of people who have read it, or have had it mentioned to them throughout the centuries have completely misunderstood it. It is said, "Steep not a kid in its mothers milk." (King James version, "Thou shalt not seethe a kid in his mothers milk." Exodus 23:19).

Unnumbered millions of people, misunderstanding this statement, to this very day in the enlightened age of 1948, will not eat any dairy products with a meat dish. It just is not done.

They think the Bible is history, and when it says, "Steep not a kid in its mother's milk," milk and the products of milk, butter and cheese, they will not take at the same time they take the kid or any kind of meat. In fact they even have separate dishes with which to cook their meat.

But you are now about to apply it psychologically. You have done your meditation and you have assumed that you are what you want to be. Consciousness is God, your attention is like the very stream of life or milk itself that nurses and makes alive that which holds your attention. In other words, what holds your attention has your life.

Throughout the centuries a kid has been used as the symbol of sacrifice. You have given birth to everything in your world. But there are things that you no longer wish to keep alive, although you have mothered and fathered them. You are a jealous father that can easily consume, like Cronus, his children. It is your right to consume what formerly you expressed when you did not know better.

Now you are detached in consciousness from that former state. It was your kid, it was your child, you embodied and expressed it in your world. But now that you have assumed that you are what you want to be, do not look back on your former state and wonder HOW it will disappear from your world. For if you look back and give attention to it, you are steeping once more that kid in its mother's milk.

Do not say to yourself, "I wonder if I am really detached from that state," or "I wonder if so and so is true." Give all your attention to the assumption that the thing is so, because all responsibility to make it so is completely removed from your shoulders. You do not have to make it so, it IS so. You appropriate what is already fact, and you walk in the assumption that it is, and in a way that you do not know, I do not know, no man knows, it becomes objectified in your world.

Do not be concerned with the how, and do not look back on your former state. "No man, having put his hand to the plow, and looking back, is fit for the kingdom of God." Luke 9:62.

Simply assume that it is done and suspend reason, suspend all the arguments of the conscious three-dimensional mind. Your desire is outside of the reach of the three-dimensional mind.

Assume you are that which you wish to be; walk as though you were it; and as you remain faithful to your assumption—it will harden into fact.

QUESTIONS AND ANSWERS

1. **Question:** *What is the meaning of the insignia on your book covers?*

   Answer: It is an eye imposed upon a heart which, in turn is imposed upon a tree laden with fruit, meaning that what you are conscious of, and accept as true, you are going to realize. As a man thinketh in his heart, so he is.

2. **Question:** *I would like to be married, but have not found the right man. How do I imagine a husband?*

   Answer: Forever in love with ideals, it is the ideal state that captures the mind. Do not confine the state of marriage to a certain man, but a full, rich and overflowing life. You desire to experience the joy of marriage. Do not modify your dream, but enhance it by making it lovelier. Then condense your desire into a single sensation, or act which implies its fulfillment.

In this western world a woman wears a wedding ring on the third finger of her left hand. Motherhood need not imply marriage; intimacy need not imply marriage, but a wedding ring does.

Relax in a comfortable arm chair, or lie flat on your back and induce a state akin to sleep. Then assume the feeling of being married. Imagine a wedding band on your finger. Touch it. Turn it around the finger. Pull it off over the knuckle. Keep the action going until the ring has the distinctness and feeling of reality. Become so lost in feeling the ring on your finger that when you open your eyes, you will be surprised that it is not there.

If you are a man who does not wear a ring, you could assume greater responsibility. How would you feel if you had a wife to care for? Assume the feeling of being a happily married man right now.

3. **Question:** *What must I do to inspire creative thoughts such as those needed for writing?*

Answer: What must you do? Assume the story has already been written and accepted by a great publishing house. Reduce the idea of being a writer to the sensation of satisfaction.

Repeat the phrase, "Isn't it wonderful!" or "Thank you, thank you, thank you," over and over again until you feel successful. Or, imagine a friend congratulating you. There are unnumbered ways of implying success, but always go to the end. Your acceptance of the end wills its fulfillment. Do not think about getting in the mood to write, but live and act as though you are now the author you desire to be. Assume you have the talent for writing. Think of the pattern you want displayed on the outside. If you write a book and no one is willing to buy it, there is no satisfaction. Act as though people are hungry for your work. Live as though you cannot produce stories, or books fast enough to meet the demand. Persist in this assumption and all that is necessary to achieve your goal will quickly burst into bloom and you will express it.

4. **Question:** *How do I imagine larger audiences for my talks?*

Answer: I can answer you best by sharing the technique used by a very able teacher I know. When this man first came to this country he began speaking in a small hall in New York City. Although only fifty or sixty people attended his Sunday morning meeting, and they sat in front, this teacher would stand at the podium and imagine a vast audience. Then he would say to the empty space, "Can you hear me back there?"

Today this man is speaking in Carnegie Hall in New York City to approximately 2,500 people every Sunday morning and Wednesday evening. He wanted to speak to crowds. He was not modest. He did not try to fool himself but built a crowd in his own consciousness, and crowds come. Stand before a large audience. Address this audience in your imagination. Feel you are on that stage and your feeling will provide the means.

5. **Question:** *Is it possible to imagine several things at the same time, or should I confine my imagining to one desire?*

    Answer: Personally I like to confine my imaginal act to a single thought, but that does not mean I will stop there. During the course of a day I may imagine many things, but instead of imagining lots of small things, I would suggest that you imagine something so big it includes all the little things. Instead of imagining wealth, health and friends, imagine being ecstatic. You could not be ecstatic and be in pain. You could not be ecstatic and be threatened with a dispossession notice. You could not be ecstatic if you were not enjoying a full measure of friendship and love.

What would the feeling be like were you ecstatic without knowing what had happened to produce your ecstasy? Reduce the idea of ecstasy to the single sensation, "Isn't it wonderful!" Do not allow the conscious, reasoning mind to ask why, because if it does it will start to look for visible causes, and then the sensation will be lost. Rather, repeat over and over again, "Isn't it wonderful!" Suspend judgment as to what is wonderful. Catch the one sensation of the wonder of it all and things will happen to bear witness to the truth of this sensation. And I promise you, it will include all the little things.

6. **Question:** *How often should I perform the imaginal act, a few days or several weeks?*

    Answer: In the Book of Genesis the story is told of Jacob wrestling with an angel. This story gives us the clue we are looking for; that when satisfaction is reached, impotence follows.

When the feeling of reality is yours, for the moment at least, you are mentally impotent. The desire to repeat the act of prayer is lost, having been replaced by the feeling of accomplishment. You cannot persist in wanting what you already have. If you assume you are what you desire to be to the point of ecstasy, you no longer want it. Your imaginal act is as much a creative act as a physical one wherein man halts, shrinks and is blessed, for as man creates his own likeness, so does your imaginal act transform itself into the likeness of your assumption. If, however, you do not reach the point of satisfaction, repeat the action over and over again until you feel as though you touched it and virtue went out of you.

7. **Question:** *I have been taught not to ask for earthly things, only for spiritual growth, yet money and things are what I need.*

Answer: You must be honest with yourself. All through Scripture the question is asked, *"What do you want of me?"* Some wanted to see, others to eat, and still others wanted to be made straight, or *"That my child live."*

Your dimensionally larger self speaks to you through the language of desire. Do not deceive yourself. Knowing what you want, claim you already have it, for it is your Father's good pleasure to give it to you and remember, what you desire, that you have.

8. **Question:** *When you have as assumed your desire, do you keep in mind the ever presence of this greater one protecting and giving you your assumption?*

    Answer: The acceptance of the end wills the means. Assume the feeling of your wish fulfilled and your dimensionally greater self will determine the means. When you appropriate a state as though you had it, the activity of the day will divert your mind from all anxious thoughts so that you do not look for signs. You do not have to carry the feeling that some presence is going to do it for you, rather you know it is already done. Knowing it is already a fact, walk as though it were, and things will happen to make it so. You do not have to be concerned about some presence doing anything for you. The deeper, dimensionally greater you has already done it. All you do is move to the place where you encounter it.

    Remember the story of the man who left the master and was on his way home when he met his servant who said, *"Your son lives."* And when he asked at what hour it was done the servant replied, *"The seventh hour."* The self-same hour that he assumed his desire, it was done for him, for it was at the seventh hour that the master said, *"Your son lives."* Your desire is already granted. Walk as though it were and, although time beats slowly in this dimension of your being, it will nevertheless bring you confirmation of your assumption. I ask you not to be impatient, though. If there is one thing you really have need of, it is patience.

9. **Question:** *Isn't there a law that says you cannot get something for nothing? Must we not earn what we desire?*
    Answer: Creation is finished! It is your Father's good pleasure to give you the kingdom. The parable of the prodigal son is your answer. In spite of man's waste, when he comes to his senses and remembers who he is, he feeds on the fatted calf of abundance and wears the robe and ring of authority. There is nothing to earn. Creation was finished in the foundation of time. You, as man, are God made visible for the purpose of displaying what is, not what is to be. Do not think you must work out your salvation by the sweat of your brow. It is not four months until the harvest, the fields are already white, simply thrust in the sickle.

10. **Question:** *Does not the thought that creation is finished rob one of his initiative?*

Answer: If you observe an event before it occurs, then the occurring event must be predetermined from the point of view of being awake in this three-dimensional world. Yet, you do not have to encounter what you observe. You can, by changing your concept of self, interfere with your future and mold it in harmony with your changed concept of self.

11. **Question:** *Does not this ability to change the future deny that creation is finished?*

Answer: No. You, by changing your concept of self, change your relationship to things. If you rearrange the words of a play to write a different one, you have not created new words, but simply had the joy of rearranging them. Your concept of self determines the order of events you encounter. They are in the foundation of the world, but not their order of arrangement.

12. **Question:** *Why should one who works hard in metaphysics always seem to lack?*

Answer: Because he has not really applied metaphysics. I am not speaking of a namby-pamby approach to life, but a daily application of the law of consciousness. When you appropriate your good, there is no need for a man, or state, to act as a medium through which your good will come.

Living in a world of men, money is needed in my every day life. If I invite you to lunch tomorrow, I must pick up the check. When I leave the hotel, I must pay the bill. In order to take the train back to New York my railway fare must be paid. I need money and it has to be there. I am not going to say, "God knows best, and He knows I need money." Rather, I will appropriate the money as though it were!

We must live boldly! We must go through life as though we possessed what we want to possess. Do not think that because you helped another, someone outside of you saw your good works and will give you something to ease your burden. There is no one to do it for you. You, yourself must go boldly on appropriating what your Father has already given you.

13. **Question:** *Can an uneducated person educate himself by assuming the feeling of being educated?*

    Answer: Yes. An aroused interest is awarded information from every side. You must sincerely desire to be well schooled. The desire to be well read, followed by the assumption that you are, makes you selective in your reading. As you progress in your education, you automatically become more selective, more discriminating in all that you do.

14. **Question:** *My husband and I are taking the class together. Should we discuss our desires with each other?*

    Answer: There are two spiritual sayings which permeate the Bible. One is, *"Go tell no man,"* and the other is *"I have told you before it comes to pass that when it does come to pass you may believe."* It takes spiritual boldness to tell another that your desire is fulfilled before it is seen on the outside. If you do not have that kind of boldness, then you had better keep quiet.

    I personally enjoy telling my plans to my wife, because we both get such a thrill when they come into being. The first person a man wants to prove this law to is his wife. It is said that Mohammad is everlastingly great because his first disciple was his wife.

15. **Question:** *Should my husband and I work on the same project or on separate ones?*

    Answer: That is entirely up to you. My wife and I have different interests, yet we have much in common. Do you recall the story I told of our return to the United States this spring? I felt it was my duty as a husband to get passage back to America, so I appropriated that to myself. I feel there are certain things that are on my wife's side of the contract, such as maintaining a clean, lovely home and finding the appropriate school for our daughter, so she takes care of those.

    Quite often my wife will ask me to imagine for her, as though she has greater faith in my ability to do it than in her own. That flatters me because every man worthy of the name wants to feel that his family has faith in him. But I see nothing wrong in the communion between two who love one another.

16. **Question:** *I would think that if you get too much into the sleepy state there would be a lack of feeling.*

    Answer: When I speak of feeling I do not mean emotion, but acceptance of the fact that the desire is fulfilled. Feeling grateful, fulfilled, or thankful, it is easy to say, "Thank You," "Isn't it wonderful!" or "It is finished." When you get into the state of thankfulness, you can either awaken knowing it is done, or fall asleep in the feeling of the wish fulfilled.

17. **Question:** *Is love a product of your own consciousness?*
Answer: All things exist in your consciousness, be they love or hate. Nothing comes from without. The hills to which you look for help are those of an inner range. Your feelings of love, hate or indifference all spring from your own consciousness. You are infinitely greater than you could ever conceive yourself to be. Never, in eternity will you reach the ultimate you. That is how wonderful you are. Love is not a product of you, you are love, for that is what God is and God's name is I am, the very name you call yourself before you make the claim as to the state you are now in.

18. **Question:** *Suppose my wants cannot materialize for six months to a year, do I wait to imagine them?*
Answer: When the desire is upon you, that is the time to accept your wish in its fullness. Perhaps there

are reasons why the urge is given you at this time. Your three-dimensional being may think it cannot be now, but your fourth dimensional mind knows it already is, so the desire should be accepted by you as a physical fact now.

Suppose you wanted to build a house. The urge to have it is now, but it is going to take time for the trees to grow and the carpenter to build the house. Although the urge seems big, do not wait to adjust to it. Claim possession now and let it objectify itself in its own strange way. Do not say it will take six months or a year. The minute the desire comes upon you, assume it is already a fact! You and you alone have given your desire a time interval and time is relative when it comes to this world. Do not wait for anything to come to pass, accept it now as though it were and see what happens.

When you have a desire, the deeper you, who men call God, is speaking. He urges you, through the language of desire, to accept that which is not that which is to be! Desire is simply his communion with you, telling you that your desire is yours, now! Your acceptance of this fact is proved by your complete adjustment to it as though it were true.

19. **Question:** *Why do some of us die young?*

    Answer: Our lives are not, in retrospect, measured by years but by the content of those years.

20. **Question:** *What would you consider a full life?*

    Answer: A variety of experiences. The more varied they are, the richer is your life. At death you function in a dimensionally larger world, and play your part on a keyboard made up of a life time of human experiences. Therefore, the more varied your experiences, the finer is your instrument and the richer is your life.

21. **Question:** *What about a child who dies at birth?*

    Answer: The child who is born, lives forever, as nothing dies. It may appear that the child who dies at birth has no keyboard of human experience but, as a poet once said:

    "He drew a circle that shut me out, Infidel, scoundrel, a thing to flout. But Love and I had the wit to win! We drew a circle that took him in."

    The loved one has access to the sensory experiences of the lover. God is love; therefore, ultimately everyone has an instrument, the keyboard of which is the sensory impressions of all men.

22. **Question:** *What is your technique of prayer?*

    Answer: It starts with desire, for desire is the mainspring of action. You must know and define your objective, then condense it into a sensation which implies fulfillment. When your desire is clearly defined, immobilize your physical body and experience, in your imagination, the action which implies its fulfillment. Repeat this act over and over again until it has the vividness and feeling of reality.

    Or, condense your desire into a single phrase that implies fulfillment such as, "Thank you Father," "Isn't it wonderful," or "It is finished." Repeat that condensed phrase, or action in your imagination over and over again. Then either awaken from that state, or slip off into the deep. It does not matter, for the act is done when you completely accept it as being finished in that sleepy, drowsy state.

23. **Question:** *Two people want the same position. One has it. The other had it and now wants it back.*

    Answer: Your Father (the dimensionally greater you) has ways and means you know not of. Accept his wisdom. Feel your desire is fulfilled, then allow your

Father to give it to you. The present one may be promoted to a higher position, or marry a man of great wealth and give up her job. She may come into a great deal of money, or choose to move to another state.

Many people say they want to work, but I question that seriously. They want security and condition security on a job. But I really do not think the average girl truly wants to get up in the morning and go to work.

24. **Question:** *What is the cause of disease and pain?*

Answer: The physical body is an emotional filter. Many human ailments, hitherto considered purely physical, are now recognized as rooted in emotional disturbances.

Pain comes from lack of relaxation. When you sleep there is no pain. If you are under an anesthetic, there is no pain because you are relaxed, as it were. If you have pain it is because you are tense and trying to force something. You cannot force an idea into embodiment, you simply appropriate it. It is attention minus effort. Only practice will bring you to that point where you can be attentive and still be relaxed.

Attention is tension toward an end, and relaxation is just the opposite. Here are two completely opposite ideas that you must blend until you learn, through practice, how to be attentive, but not tense. The word "contention" means "attention minus effort." In the state of contention you are held by the idea without tension.

25. **Question:** *No matter how much I try to be happy, underneath, I have a melancholy feeling of being left out. Why?*

Answer: Because you feel you are not wanted. Were I you, I would assume I am wanted. You know the technique. The assumption that you are wanted may seem false when first assumed, but if you will feel wanted and respected, and persist in that assumption, you will be amazed how others will seek you out. They will begin to see qualities in you they had never seen before. I promise you. If you will but assume you are wanted, you will be.

26. **Question:** *If security came to me through the death of a loved one, did I bring about that death?*

Answer: Do not think for one second that you brought about a death by assuming security. The greater you is not going to injure any one. It sees all and, knowing the length of life of all, it can inspire the other to give you that which can fulfill your assumption.

You did not kill the person who named you in his will. If, a few days after your complete acceptance of the idea of security, Uncle John made his exit from this three-dimensional plane and left you his estate, it is only because it was time for Uncle John to go. He did not die one second before his time, however. The greater you saw the life span of John and used him as the way to bring about the fulfillment of your feeling of security.

The acceptance of the end wills the means toward the fulfillment of that end. Do not be concerned with anything save the end. Always bear in mind that the responsibility to make it so is completely removed from your shoulders. It is yours because you accept it as so!

27. **Question:** *I have more than one objective. Would it be ineffective to concentrate on different objectives at different periods of concentration?*

    Answer: I like to take one consuming ambition, restrict it to a single short phrase, or act that implies fulfillment, but I do not limit my ambition. I only know that my real objective will include all the little ones.

28. **Question:** *I find it difficult to change my concept of self.
    Why?*

    Answer: Because your desire to change has not
    been aroused. If you would fall in love with what
    you really want to be, you would become it. It takes
    an intense hunger to bring about a transformation
    of self.

    *"As the hart panteth after the waterbrooks, so pan-
    teth my soul after thee, O Lord."* If you would become
    as thirsty for perfection as the little hart is for water
    that it braves the anger of the tiger in the forest, you
    would become perfect.

29. **Question:** *I am contemplating a business venture. It
    means a great deal to me, but I cannot imagine how it
    can come into being.*

    Answer: You are relieved of that responsibility. You
    do not have to make it a reality, it already is! Although
    your concept of self seems so far removed from the
    venture you now contemplate, it exists now as a real-
    ity within you. Ask yourself how you would feel and
    what you would be doing if your business venture
    were a great success. Become identified with that

character and feeling and you will be amazed how quickly you will realize your dream.

The only sacrifice you are called upon to make, is to give up your present concept of self and appropriate the desire you want to express.

30. **Question:** *As a metaphysical student I have been taught to believe that race beliefs and universal assumptions affect me. Do you mean that only to the degree I give these universal beliefs power over me, am I influenced by them?*

Answer: Yes. It is only your individual viewpoint, as your world is forever bearing witness to your present concept of self. If someone offends you, change your concept of self. That is the only way others change. Tonight's paper may be read by any six people in this room and no two will interpret the same story in the same way. One will be elated, the other depressed, another indifferent, and so on, yet it is the same story.

Universal assumptions, race beliefs, call them what you will, they are not important to you. What is important is your concept, not of another, but of yourself, for the concept you hold of yourself determines the concept you hold of others. Leave others alone. What are they to you? Follow your own desires.

The law is always in operation, always absolute. Your consciousness is the rock upon which all structures rest. Watch what you are aware of. You need not concern yourself with others because you are sustained by the absoluteness of this law. No man comes to you of his own accord, be he good, bad or indifferent. He did not choose you! You chose him! He was drawn to you because of what you are.

You cannot destroy the state another represents through force. Rather, leave him alone. What is he to you? Rise to a higher level of consciousness and you will find a new world awaiting you, and as you sanctify yourself, others are sanctified.

31. **Question:** *Who wrote the Bible?*

Answer: The Bible was written by intelligent men who used solar and phallic myths to reveal psychological truths. But we have mistaken their allegory for history and, therefore, have failed to see their true message.

It is strange, but when the Bible was launched upon the world, and acceptance seemed to be in sight, the great Alexandria Library was burnt to the ground, leaving no record as to how the Bible came into being. Few people can read other languages, so they cannot compare their beliefs with others. Our churches do not encourage us to compare. How many of the millions who accept the Bible as fact, ever question it? Believing it is the word of God, they blindly accept the words and thus lose the essence they contain. Having accepted the vehicle, they do not understand what the vehicle conveys.

32. **Question:** *Do you use the Apocrypha?*

Answer: Not in my teaching. I have several volumes of them at home. They are no greater than the sixty-six books of our present Bible. They are simply telling the same truth in a different way. For instance, the story is told of Jesus, as a young boy, watching children make birds out of mud. Holding the birds in their hands, they pretend the birds are flying. Jesus approaches and knocks the birds out of their hands. As they begin to cry, he picks up one of the broken birds and remolds it. Holding it high, he breaths upon it and the bird takes wing.

Here is a story of one who came to break the idols in the minds of men, then show them how to use the same substance and remold it into a beautiful form and give it life. That is what this story is trying to convey. *"I come, not to bring peace, but a sword."* Truth slays all the little mud hens of the mind; slays illusions and then re-molds them into a new pattern which sets man free.

33. **Question:** *If Jesus was a fictional character created by Biblical writers for the purpose of illustrating certain psychological dramas, how do you account for the fact that he and his philosophy are mentioned in the nonreligious and non-Christian history of those times? Were not Pontius Pilate and Herod real flesh and blood Roman officials in those days?*

Answer: The story of Jesus is the identical story as that of the Hindu savior, Krishna. They are the same psychological characters. Both were supposed to have been born of virgin mothers. The rulers of the time sought to destroy them when they were children. Both healed the sick, resurrected the dead, taught the gospel of love and died a martyr's death for mankind. Hindus and Christians alike believe their savior to be God made man.

Today people quote Socrates, yet the only proof that Socrates ever existed is in the works of Plato. It is said that Socrates drank hemlock, but I ask you, who is Socrates? I once quoted a line from Shakespeare and a lady said to me, "But Hamlet said that." Hamlet never said it, Shakespeare wrote the lines and put the words in the mouth of a character he created and named Hamlet. St. Augustine once said, "That which is now called the Christian religion existed among the ancients. They began to call Christianity the true religion, yet it never existed."

34. Question: *Do you use affirmations and denials?*

Answer: Let us leave these schools of thought that use affirmations and denials. The best affirmation, and the only effective one is an assumption which, in itself implies denial of the former state.

The best denial is total indifference. Things wither and die through indifference. They are kept alive through attention. You do not deny a thing by saying it does not exist. Rather you put feeling into it by recognizing it, and what you recognize as true, is true to you, be it good, bad or indifferent.

35. Question: *Is it possible for one to appear dead and still not be dead?*

Answer: General Lee was supposed to have been born two years after his mother, believed to be dead, was buried alive. Lucky for her she was not embalmed or buried in the earth, but in a vault where someone heard her cry and released her. Two years later Mrs. Lee bore a son who became General Lee. That is part of this country's history.

36. **Question:** *How could one who was deprived in his youth become a success in life?*

Answer: We are creatures of habit, forming patterns of the mind which repeat themselves over and over again. Although habit acts like a compelling law which drives one to repeat the patterns, it is not a law, for you and I can change the patterns. Many successful men such as Henry Ford, Rockefeller and Carnegie were deprived in their youth. Many of the great names in this country came from poor families, yet they left behind them great accomplishments in the political, artistic and financial world.

One evening a friend of mine attended a meeting for young advertising executives. The speaker of the evening said to these young men: "I have but one thing to say to you tonight and that is to make yourself big and you cannot fail."

Taking an ordinary fish bowl, he filled it with two bags, one of English walnuts and the other of small beans. Mixing them with his hand, he began to shake the bowl and said, "This bowl is life. You cannot stop its shaking as life is a constant pulsing, living rhythm, but watch." And as they watched the big walnuts came to the top of the bowl as the little beans fell to the bottom.

Looking into the bowl the man asked, "Which one of you is complaining, asking why?" Then added, "Isn't it strange, the sound is coming from the bowl and not the outside. A bean is complaining that if he had had the same environment as the walnut he, too would do big things, but he never had the chance." Then he took a little bean from the bottom of the bowl and placed him on top saying, "I can move the bean through sheer force, but I cannot stop the bowl of life from shaking," and as he shook the bowl, the little bean once again slid to the bottom.

Hearing another voice of complaint he asked, "What's that I hear? You are saying that I should take one of those big fellows who thinks he is so big and put him on the bottom and see what happens to him? You believe he will be just as limited as you because he will be robbed of the opportunity of big things just as you are? Let's see."

Then the speaker took one of the big walnuts and pushed him right down to the bottom of the bowl saying, "I still can't stop the bowl from shaking," and as the men watched the big walnut came to the top again. Then the speaker added:

> *"Gentlemen, if you really want to be successful in life, make yourself big."*

My friend took this message to heart and began to assume he was a successful businessman. Today he is truly a big man if you judge success by dollars. He now employs over a thousand people in the city of New York. Each one of you can do what he did. Assume you are what you want to be. Walk in that assumption and it will harden into fact.

ABOUT THE AUTHOR

Neville Goddard was born on 19 February 1905 in St. Michael, Barbados in the British West Indies, to Joseph Nathaniel Goddard, a merchant, and Wilhelmina Nee Hinkinson.

In 1922 he came to the United States to study drama at the age of seventeen. He became a dancer, and during this time, married his first wife. Together, they had a son named Joseph Neville Goddard. While touring with his dance company in England he developed an interest in metaphysics after striking up a conversation with a Scotsman who lent him a series of books on the powers of the mind. Upon his return to New York he gave up the entertainment industry to devote his full attention to the study of spiritual and mystical matters.

Neville Goddard's first marriage was short lived, and he remained single for years until he met his second wife in the 1930s. After they married, they had a daughter named Victoria or "Vicky". In 1943, he was drafted into the U.S. Army at age 38, but felt that he was too old to become a soldier and was anxious about leaving his wife and daughter at home. Through the power of imagination, as Neville told it in his March 24, 1972 lecture, he was honorably discharged after just a few weeks of training. One consequence of his brief Army training was that he received full United States citizenship upon his discharge, having been a British citizen up until that point.

Neville wrote more than ten books and was a popular speaker on metaphysical themes from the late 1930s until his death in 1972.

NOTES